Variation Theory and Second Language Acquisition

H.D. Adamson

Georgetown University Press, Washington, D.C.

Permission for the use of figures in this book is hereby gratefully acknowledged:

Figure 1.1: Figure 14 in Roger Brown, A first language. Cambridge, Mass.: Harvard University Press. Reprinted by permission. Figures 3.1a, 3.1b, 6.3: Tables 8, 9, 10, respectively, in Roger W. Anderson, ed., Second language acquisition research. Rowley, Mass.: Newbury House. Reprinted with permission of the editor.

Library of Congress Cataloging-in-Publication Data

Adamson, H.D. (Hugh Douglas)
    Variation theory and second language acquisition / H.D. Adamson.
    p.   cm.
    Bibliography: p.
    ISBN 0-87840-215-2 (pbk.) :
    1. Language and languages--Variation. 2. Second language acquisition. 3. Psycholinguistics. I. Title.
P120.V37A33 1988   87-34198
401'.9--dc19   CIP

CONTENTS

Preface   v

1 Language Universals and Implicational Hierarchies   1

   1 Morpheme acquisition studies   1
   2 Universals   4
   3 Modeling language acquisition   5

2 Variation Theory   9

   1 Linguistic continua   9
   2 The wave model   11
   3 Linguistic environment   13
   4 Implicational tables   13
   5 The wave model in second language acquisition   16
   6 Variable rules   18

3 Pidgins, Creoles, and Interlanguages   22

   1 Pidgins and creoles   22
   2 Bickerton's theory of pidginization   23
   3 Universals in pidginization   24
   4 The nativization hypothesis   26
   5 An invariant continuum   28
   6 Linguistic variables and social variables   31

4 An Experimental Study of Bickerton's
   Bioprogram Theory Applied to
   Second Language Acquisition   34

   1 Bickerton's theory of universals   34
   2 The specific-nonspecific distinction   35
   3 The experiment   38

iii

5 Linguistic Rules and Psychological Reality   43

   1   Linguistics and psychology   43
   2   Declarative knowledge and procedural knowledge   47
   3   Competence rules, performance rules, and
       productions   49
   4   Evidence for psychological reality   52
   5   Summary   53

6 The Psychological Reality of Variable Rules   54

   1   The necessity of variable rules   54
   2   The psycholinguistic correlates of constraints   55

7 Prototypes and Variable Rules   64

   1   A prototype morphological category   64
   2   Prototype syntactic categories   68
   3   The acquisition of a syntactic category   70
   4   A prototype semantic category   75
   5   Conclusion   77

8 Variation Theory and the Monitor Model   78

   1   Krashen's theory of monitoring   78
   2   Monitoring and language change   80
   3   Krashen's model versus Labov's model   81
   4   The bootstrap hypothesis   84

References   87

PREFACE

1. Rationale for the book. Since Chomsky's <u>Aspects of a Theory of Syntax</u> was published in 1965, linguistics has developed in several new directions. Three important new movements are in the areas of psycholinguistics, sociolinguistics and applied linguistics. The first of these studies how human beings (and lately, gorillas and chimpanzees) acquire and mentally process language. The second analyzes speech patterns in the community, such as regional and social dialects. And the third looks at second language acquisition with a view toward developing better teaching techniques. The three subdisciplines have shared much with one another, but perhaps their most important common element, the one that sets them apart from the parent discipline of theoretical linguistics, is their use of language performance data, the actual speech and writing of language users. Theoretical linguistics, on the other hand, uses as data the intuitions of individual scholars about whether particular sentences are grammatical.

In spite of their common interest in speech data, scholars in the three subdisciplines have, unfortunately, not kept in close touch with each other. This was not always true. In the 1970s, applied linguists were very familiar with the work of psycholinguists. It was logical that the young discipline, second language scholarship, should look to the older discipline, first language scholarship, for theories and methods. For this reason, the initial second language studies simply reproduced first language studies, substituting second language learners for first language learners as subjects. During this early period, the two disciplines asked the same kinds of questions: In what order are certain language structures acquired? What is the role of simplified input in acquisition? In addition, applied linguists borrowed constructs and hypotheses from psycholinguists--for example, the Language Acquisition Device, and the notion that certain linguistic structures are universally more natural. The result of this close connection between disciplines has been the discovery that there are important similarities in the processes of first and second language acquisition.

However, in the 1980s, as the discipline of applied linguistics has matured, a second generation of scholars has emerged. These scholars have discovered that insights into the process of second language acquisition can be gained not only from first language studies, but also

v

from studies of nonstandard dialects, and pidgin and creole languages. These subjects are the traditional concern of sociolinguists, and as a result applied linguists, especially in Europe, have increasingly borrowed theoretical constructs and analytic tools from sociolinguists. Most sociolinguistic studies of native speakers have been done within the framework of 'variation theory', which was developed by William Labov in the 1960s. Variation theory provides analytic techniques for discovering systematic relations within highly variable data. Therefore, the theory is very useful for studying language varieties that contain much variation, such as nonstandard dialects, pidgin and creole languages, and, of course, the speech of second language learners. However, it has not been clear within applied linguistics how the new theoretical paradigm borrowed from variation theory relates to the old, but still robust, paradigm borrowed from psycholinguistics. The result has been confusion about how to integrate the new with the old.

In fact, the relationship of sociolinguistics to psycholinguistics has been unclear not just within the field of second language acquisition but in general. In an influential article in Language in Society, Kay and McDaniel (1979) attempted to assess the psychological implications of variation theory, and concluded that these implications were not clear at present. In a reply to Kay and McDaniel in the same journal, Sankoff and Labov (1979) attempted to spell out more clearly the psychological claims of variable rules, but this reply was only a first step toward a complete theory and many questions remained. In the final installment of this exchange, Kay and McDaniel (1981) concluded that variation theory was at a crossroads, similar to the state of astronomy just before Copernicus. Variationists know that their work has relevance to psycholinguistics, but they are not sure exactly what that relevance is. Since Kay and McDaniel's pessimistic assessment of the possibility of a rapprochement between sociolinguistics and psycholinguistics, the two disciplines have not come closer together. Sociolinguists have typically been concerned to gather new data that lead to a greater understanding of language use and change within the community. Unanswered questions concerning the psychological relevance of their work are not especially troubling to them; they can afford to wait until more is known in all areas of linguistics before sorting out the psychological relevance of their work.

Applied linguists, on the other hand, cannot afford to wait. They need at least the beginnings of a unifying theory because their discipline is firmly grounded in psychological concerns but is rapidly adopting sociolinguistic methods. Lacking some notion of the psychological relevance of sociolinguistic constructs and tools such as implicational scales, variable rules, and monitoring, the field is in danger of being split into two camps -- psycholinguists and sociolinguists, who both study second language acquisition, but who are unable to integrate their findings. This book is, I hope, a first step toward such a unifying theory.

2. Organization of the book. The argument of the book might logically be divided into three parts. The first section (Chapters 1 through 4) shows how variation theory, which was developed to study the speech of native speakers, has been used to study the speech of language learners. Chapter 1 begins with a review of the classic morpheme acquisition studies of the 1970s by Brown and by Dulay and Burt. This material will be familiar to all readers, but I have attempted to interpret it in variationist terms, pointing out how the psycholinguists' 'rank orders' are a form of the variationists' 'implicational hierarchies'. Chapter 2 explains variation theory and its most widely used analytical technique: implicational hierarchies and variable rules. Chapters 3 and 4 examine the similarities in second language speech and pidgin and creole languages, pointing out how all three varieties may arise from similar psycholinguistic processes.

The second section of the book (Chapters 5, 6, and 7) explores the psychological relevance of variation theory. Chapter 5 lays the groundwork for this discussion by examining the psychological significance of any linguistic theory. This discussion necessarily leads to a discussion of the basic assumptions of Chomskian linguistics, including the widely misunderstood competence-performance distinction. In addition, the relationship of Chomskian linguistics to psycholinguistics and artificial intelligence is explained, and all three disciplines are situated within the emerging field of cognitive science, an overarching discipline within which second language scholarship is beginning to take its place. Chapter 6 shows why variable rules are necessary in a psychologically real theory of language acquisition and suggests a psychological interpretation of these rules. Chapter 7 shows how variable rules are related to mental prototypes, the study of which is one of the most robust areas of cognitive psychology.

The third part of the book (Chapter 8) shows the relationship of variation theory to Stephen Krashen's famous Monitor Model. Any book on second language acquisition must take Krashen's theory into account, but variation theory is especially relevant to his ideas. This is because Krashen got his ideas about monitoring from William Labov's classic studies of variation in the speech community, which are discussed in Chapter 2. But Krashen's theory of monitoring and Labov's theory of monitoring do not appear to be compatible, and this incompatibility has puzzled scholars (especially Tarone 1979, 1985) for some time. After comparing the two monitor models, and analyzing some recent data on monitoring by second language learners, I suggest an alternative theory of monitoring, which combines Labov's and Krashen's insights.

3. Acknowledgments. This book has been long in the writing and my family, friends, and colleagues have been long suffering. Very special thanks are due to my wife Alice and to my daughters (and sometimes subjects) Marie and Katie. Thanks to friends and colleagues who commented on portions of the manuscript (but whose good advice was not always heeded): Ceil Lucas, Ralph Fasold, William Labov, and Jim Sanford. Thanks to Virginia Collier, Henry Hamburger, Dee Holisky, Emmett Holman, and Leonard Talmy for helpful and most enjoyable discussions. Thanks to Jeff Hammond and Dave Kuebrich for editorial suggestions and for friendship. Thanks to my students, who worked with me through difficult theoretical material when what they really needed to talk about was what to do in class on Monday. Thanks to the Mellon Foundation for a postdoctoral fellowship to the University of Pennsylvania which enabled me to complete this work.

H.D.A.
Annandale, Virginia
1986

Chapter 1

LANGUAGE UNIVERSALS
AND IMPLICATIONAL HIERARCHIES

1. Morpheme acquisition studies. A good place to begin a discussion of modern language acquisition scholarship is Roger Brown's (1973) study of how three American children acquired English during their second and third years. Brown and his colleagues sat down with the children and their parents for about half an hour every one or two weeks and tape recorded what the children and parents said; then they analyzed how the children's English emerged. In particular, Brown looked at 14 function words and inflections which he called 'grammatical morphemes'. These included the, a, in, on, plural -s, and others (a complete list appears in Figure 1.1). Brown wanted to find out in which order these morphemes were learned. For this he used the concept of 'obligatory context', a linguistic environment where adult usage requires the morpheme. For example, (1) contains an obligatory context for the plural morpheme.

(1)   I have three block __.

Brown counted all the obligatory contexts for an individual morpheme--say, the progressive -ing--that occurred during a taping session. Then he counted the number of tokens of -ing actually uttered in those contexts. He could then calculate the percentage of correct usage by dividing the number of tokens by the number of obligatory contexts. For example, if his subject Sarah supplied plural -s 20 times during a taping session, but should have supplied it 40 times, the percentage of accurate usage was 50 percent. Naturally, at first the children's percentage of accurate usage was often zero because they did not yet use the required morpheme. But, gradually the morphemes emerged.

Sarah's acquisition of the -ing morpheme is charted in Figure 1.2. The learning curve in Figure 1.2 is not the gradual upward slope that can be found in many learning studies; instead, the line 'swoops and jags' all over the chart. This unevenness is probably due to the small number of obligatory contexts in each taping session. Notice, though,

1

that by the tenth taping session the line begins to even out at about 90 percent accuracy. At this point, Sarah had virtually acquired the -ing morpheme. When a subject used a morpheme with 90 percent accuracy for three consecutive taping sessions, Brown considered that the morpheme had been acquired. He then ranked the 14 morphemes in the order in which they were acquired by the three children. These orders of acquisition appear in Figure 1.1, which also shows the children's stage of development when the morphemes were acquired. The five stages of development, indicated by roman numerals I-V, are determined by calculating the child's mean length of utterance (MLU)--the average number of morphemes in the child's utterances. For example, stage II begins when the MLU reaches 2.25 morphemes per utterance. Figure 1.1 shows that the child's developmental stage (and MLU) is a much better predictor of when a morpheme will be acquired than is the child's age.

Figure 1.1 The order of acquisition of 14 grammatical morphemes by Brown's three children. The numbers in parentheses indicate the child's age in (years;months).

Adam		Sarah		Eve	
I (2;3)		I (2;3)		I (1;6)	
II (2;6)	Present progressive, in, on, plural	II (2;10)	Plural	II (1;9)	
			in, on		
			Present progressive, past irregular, Possessive		Present progressive, on
III (2;11)	Uncontractible copula, past irregular	III (3;1)	Uncontractible copula, Articles	III (1;11)	in
					Plural, possessive
IV (3;2)	Articles, Third person irregular, possessive	IV (3;8)	Third person regular	IV (2;2)	Past regular
V (3;6)	Third person regular, Past regular, Uncontractible auxiliary, Contractible copula, Contractible auxiliary	V (4;0)	Past regular, Uncontractible auxiliary, Contractible copula, Third person irregular, Contractible auxiliary	V (2;3)	Uncontractible copula, Past irregular, Articles, Third person regular, Third person irregular, Uncontractible auxiliary, Contractible copula, Contractible auxiliary

The acquisition orders for Sarah, Adam and Eve shown in Figure 1.1 are similar in several ways. The present progressive -ing is acquired early: first for Adam and Eve, third for Sarah. The contractible auxiliary (Aux) is last for all three children. But there are some differences in the acquisition orders, too: Eve acquires the regular past morpheme sixth; Sarah, ninth; Adam, eleventh. Brown wanted to know if there was a basic similarity in the three acquisition orders or if the apparent similarity was due to chance. Applying the Spearman rank-order correlation test, he found that it was highly unlikely that the similarities could have occurred by chance. He concluded that the acquisition of these morphemes was not random but systematic for these children and perhaps for all children.

Figure 1.2   Sarah's acquisition of -ing morpheme.

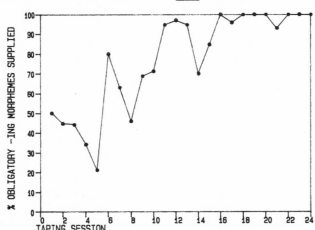

Brown's claim that children acquire certain English morphemes in roughly the same order was supported by de Villiers and de Villiers' (1973) study of 21 children from 16 to 40 months of age. The de Villiers' study was cross-sectional, and since they did not follow their subjects' morpheme acquisition over time, the de Villiers had to calculate the order of acquisition in a different way than did Brown. In fact, they used two methods for measuring the acquisition order. The first method was simply to calculate the percentage of each morpheme supplied in obligatory contexts by all of the subjects. This method answered the question: which morpheme was used most accurately by all the subjects? Which was next? And so on. As noted below, this method does not really measure the morpheme acquisition order but rather the overall accuracy of morpheme use. The second method was to find the lowest MLU at which each morpheme was supplied at 90 percent accuracy by any subject. This method answered the question: which morpheme was supplied at 90 percent accuracy at the lowest developmental level (as measured by MLU) by any subject? which was next? and so on. Brown (1973) compared the two rank orders the de Villiers had found with the average rank order for his subjects and found an amazing degree of similarity. Thus, the de Villiers'

experiment verified that Brown had, as he claimed, discovered 'a developmental phenomenon of substantial generality' (Brown 1973:274).

Morpheme studies were soon undertaken by second language researchers. In a cross-sectional study, Dulay and Burt (1974) studied 55 Chinese speaking and 60 Spanish-speaking children, ages 6-8. They focused on 11 of the morphemes studied by Brown. Unfortunately, it was not possible for Dulay and Burt to use the second of the de Villiers' methods for measuring the order of morpheme acquisition because in second language acquisition there is no good independent measure of language development like the MLU. Unlike first language learners, second language learners do not go through a one-word stage and then a two-word stage, but often produce multiword utterances from the beginning. So instead of correlating morpheme accuracy with the MLU, Dulay and Burt used only the first of the de Villiers' methods: they measured the overall morpheme accuracy for all of their subjects. For this reason their study was not, strictly speaking, a morpheme acquisition study but a morpheme accuracy study. Dulay and Burt found an order of morpheme accuracy that was somewhat similar to Brown's order of morpheme acquisition, but not similar enough to be statistically significant. In addition, Dulay and Burt discovered a remarkable fact: the morpheme accuracy order of the Spanish-speaking children correlated significantly with the accuracy order of the Chinese-speaking children. Assuming that the order of accuracy reflects the order of acquisition, Dulay and Burt claimed to have found a natural order of morpheme acquisition that was relatively independent of the learners' first language. This was astonishing to second language scholars, who had assumed that the main influence on the development of a second language was the learner's first language.

What accounts for the natural orders of morpheme accuracy/acquisition? Behaviorist psychology suggests that learners will first master those morphemes they hear most frequently, so Brown checked to see if the children's acquisition orders correlated with how often these forms were used by their parents. He found no correlation and concluded that the acquisition order could only be explained by the semantic and syntactic complexity of the morphemes. This explanation implies that certain linguistic structures are universally 'simpler' than others and therefore easier for human beings to acquire. We will now consider some theories about how notions of universal simplicity may play a part in first language acquisition, as Brown's study suggests.

2. Universals. Chomsky (1965) proposed a strong theory of universals in language acquisition, claiming that children are born with specific linguistic knowledge, which is contained in a language acquisition device (LAD). Chomsky's discussion of innate knowledge is extremely technical, so I will not consider one of his examples, but rather an example proposed by Bickerton (1981).[1] Bickerton notes that the English progressive morpheme -ing is easily acquired. Brown's subjects acquired it first and apparently never used it incorrectly; at first these subjects omitted -ing, but the morpheme emerged only in obligatory contexts, not in inappropriate ones. The function of the -ing morpheme is to differentiate stative and nonstative verbs since only nonstatives freely take the progressive aspect, as shown in (2)-(5).

(2)   Edna is hitting Sally. (nonstative)
(3)   The basement was leaking. (nonstative)
(4)   *George is being tall. (stative)
(5)   *Sally is knowing George. (stative)

Bickerton also notes that the stative-nonstative distinction (SND) is marked in all creole languages. He concludes that humans instinctively know the difference between a state and an action and so are especially attuned to picking up how a verb system marks this distinction. Therefore, it is easier for language learners to acquire progressive -ing than to acquire, say, the regular past tense marker, which does not correspond to an innately known distinction.

A second theory of how universals work in acquisition is Traugott's (1977) idea of natural semantax. She claims that children are born with natural language production strategies so that certain phonological and semantic-syntactic structures are easier to produce--are simpler--than others. Natural patterns are acquired early and are widespread among the languages of the world. She notes that Stampe (1969) provides an account of naturalness in phonology which is based on the assumption that sound change is physiologically and psychologically motivated. For all children, consonants tend to be voiceless because of constriction; vowels tend to be voiced because of a lack of constriction. Furthermore, according to Drachman (cited in Traugott 1977:137), it is simpler to produce successive consonants in a word in successively more retracted positions according to the hierarchy p-t-k. This results in metathesis, as when a child pronounces alligator [daeg]; animal [maenu]; coffee [baki]. Clearly, simplifications such as these must be abandoned if the child is to communicate, so the child elaborates the system. According to Traugott, a natural hierarchy of difficulty exists for syntax and semantics as well as for phonology. For example, Keenan and Comrie (1977) claim that relative clauses with subject focus (The woman **who** met you is my wife) are less marked ('simpler') than those with direct object focus (The woman **whom** you met is my wife); both of these are less marked than relative clauses with indirect object focus (The woman to **whom** you spoke is my wife). As Traugott observes (1977:139): 'We would predict that, where material from other structures does not interfere, the usual order of acquisition would be from least to most marked.'

Theories of language universals suggest that first language acquisition is, to some extent, not random but systematic and developmental. Perhaps all children pass through similar stages of language development just as they pass through similar stages of motor coordination--first lifting the head, then turning over, then crawling--and just as they pass through Piaget's stages of cognitive development. Many researchers believe that language universals play a role in second language acquisition as well. Some of the evidence for this belief is reviewed in Chapters 3 and 4.

3. Modeling language acquisition. If there is a natural path of first and second language acquisition, it should be possible to place learners' developing idiolects along a continuum ranging from simple varieties to complex varieties. To see what such a developmental continuum might look like, we must examine more closely the analytical methods used by Brown and by Dulay and Burt. These researchers faced the problem of analyzing the miasma of variation in the speech of two-year-olds and second language learners. One way of dealing with variation is to ignore it by abstracting away from individual subjects' data to create an idealized system. This is the course taken by Saussure and by Chomsky in their descriptions of adult native-speaker speech. Saussure attempted to describe 'langue', that part of speech which is shared by all speakers of the speech community. Langue is a social, not an individual, phenomenon, and is therefore highly abstract. Chomsky desired to study language from an individual-psychological perspective, but did away with variation by positing an 'ideal speaker-hearer' who learned language instantaneously. Clearly, neither Saussure's nor Chomsky's abstractions are very helpful to scholars studying the highly variable utterances of actual learners, a point developed further in Chapter 6.

Brown and Dulay and Burt were able to find patterns in variable data by using the technique of rank ordering, where language structures are arranged so that if an individual has structure number 2, she will have structure number 1 as well. In Brown's study, for example, if a child has acquired the plural morpheme, one can predict that she will also have acquired the progressive -ing morpheme. A rank order such as Brown's morpheme acquisition order is an implicational hierarchy, an extremely useful device for analyzing variable data as long as several points are kept in mind. First, when an implicational hierarchy is constructed from the data of a group of subjects, it does not necessarily fit every individual in the group. Brown constructed an average order of acquisition hierarchy for his three subjects, where -ing was ranked first and plural was ranked fourth. This ranking implies that if a child has acquired the plural, she has acquired -ing. But as Figure 1.1 shows, this implication is true only for Adam and Eve, not for Sarah. However, Brown's statistical tests show that the hierarchies of individual subjects are significantly similar, so the average hierarchy is not too different from the individual hierarchies. Constructing an average order of acquisition requires abstracting away from the speech data of individuals, and in this sense it is like describing langue, or the competence of the ideal speaker-hearer. However, such abstracting is commonly done in psychological studies involving groups, and it results in a description that is closer to the actual speech data than are the very abstract descriptions of Saussure and Chomsky.

A second point is that whereas in Brown's study one can compare the acquisition orders of individuals to make sure they are significantly similar to the average order, in Dulay and Burt's study this comparison cannot be made because they did not compute individual accuracy orders--they just lumped all the data together. Dulay and Burt have been criticized for this lack by Rosansky (1976) and by Anderson (1977). But Dulay and Burt's order has been replicated in so many studies (Bailey et al. 1974; Fathman; 1975; Krashen et al. 1976) that most scholars agree that Dulay and Burt, like Brown, discovered a phenomenon of some generality.

A third point to be kept in mind when working with implicational hierarchies or rank orders is that they incorrectly suggest that morphemes are acquired one after another at even intervals. Figure 1.1 shows that this is not true. For example, Adam acquired the plural morpheme and <u>on</u> at about the same time, but there was a long gap before he acquired the next morpheme, uncontractible copula. Dulay and Burt reanalyzed their data in order to construct a hierarchy that did not contain this false implication. Their results are shown in Figure 1.3, where morphemes of about equal accuracy are grouped together.

Since Dulay and Burt's studies, implicational hierarchies have been found in areas of interlanguage other than grammatical morphemes. For example, in a longitudinal study of six Spanish speakers, Cazden et al. (1975) found four stages in the acquisition of English negation. These stages are shown in Figure 1.4. The stage model in Figure 1.4 is an implicational hierarchy, but it is different from a rank order in three respects. First, Cazden et al.'s study focused on a single structure (in this case a syntactic, not a morphological one) rather than on several different structures. Second, Cazden et al. studied the development of the negative from the time it emerged until the time it closely resembled the native speaker form; thus their study is truly developmental.

Figure 1.3   Acquisition hierarchy for 13 English grammatical morphemes for Spanish-speaking and Cantonese-speaking children.

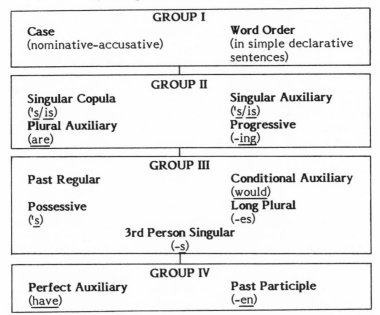

Brown and Dulay and Burt, on the other hand, studied only the adult or native speaker forms--the final products of the acquisition process. These differences imply a third difference: in Brown's and Dulay and

Burt's hierarchies the presence of the second ranked structure implies the presence of the first ranked structure, but in Cazden et al.'s stage model this is not so. The stage II structure implies that the stage I structure was once present, but it may have disappeared by the end of stage II.

Figure 1.4   Stages in the acquisition of the English negative by six Spanish speakers.

Stage	Syntactic Form	Examples
1	<u>no</u> + V	I no can see.
		They have no water.
2	<u>don't</u> + V	I don't can explain.
		He don't like it.
3	Aux + Neg	Somebody is not coming.
		He can't see.
4	analyzed <u>don't</u>	It doesn't spin.
		I didn't know.

Another study which discovered an implicational hierarchy in the acquisition of a second language was made by the ZISA group (Meisel, Clahson, and Pienemann 1981; Meisel 1983), who looked at the acquisition of German by adult speakers of Spanish and Italian. They discovered that their subjects learned German word order rules not   just in a similar order but in an invariant order. These findings are discussed in Chapter 3.

The discovery of implicational hierarchies in language acquisition data gives support to the notion of an acquisition continuum, a series of stages through which many learners (or in the case of the ZISA group's subjects, all learners) pass on their way to acquiring a first or a second language, guided by innate strategies and perhaps by innate linguistic knowledge. Rank orders and stage models are two kinds of implicational hierarchies that are useful for analyzing this continuum. However, these and other tools of variation study have been most highly developed by linguists who study not learners but adult native speakers. These sociolinguistic studies are considered in the next chapter.

Note

1. Bickerton's universals are different from Chomsky's in at least two ways. First, Bickerton calls his universals 'cognitive' universals rather than 'language universals' because they stem from knowledge about how the world works, not just knowledge about how language works. This point is discussed in Chapter 4. Second, Bickerton's universals are not marked in all languages. Rather, they are statistical universals; languages have a tendency to mark them.

Chapter 2

VARIATION THEORY

'Interlanguage' is the speech of second language learners. The term suggests that this speech is systematic and rule governed, like other forms of language. When Selinker (1972) introduced the term, he claimed only that the speech of a single second language speaker was systematic, not that the same system was shared by a group of speakers. Each learner spoke an 'idiosyncratic dialect' that changed and developed until it closely resembled the target language. But as we have seen, researchers have discovered similar patterns in the speech of many L2 learners. Cazden et al. (1975) found that Spanish speakers learning English passed through the same stages of negative formation. They found similarities in other linguistic subsystems as well, such as question formation. In addition, Dulay and Burt (1974) found patterns of acquisition in the speech of children from two very different native language backgrounds: Chinese and Spanish. It is still not clear how widespread these patterns are, because neither Cazden et al. nor Dulay and Burt used tests of statistical significance in the rigorous way that Brown did. The ZISA group, on the other hand, discovered an invariant order of acquisition of German word order rules. These studies and others suggest that there are patterns of acquisition—an interlanguage—that are shared by many learners, even though the dissimilarities among speakers may outweigh the similarities.

1. **Linguistic continua.** As noted in Chapter 1, language acquisition researchers have used implicational hierarchies in one form or another to display interlanguage patterns. These implicational hierarchies claim that interlanguage structures can be arranged along a continuum so that learners will first use structure x, then structure y, and so on. A hierarchical arrangement of interlanguage structures forms a continuum ranging from simple to complex, as we have seen. Continua can also be found in adult native speaker speech where they have been used by sociolinguists to study the variation in regional and social dialects. In fact, implicational hierarchies are just one of the tools sociolinguists use to discover patterns in variable linguistic data; other tools include the wave model, the cross products chart, and the variable rule. This

chapter discusses how sociolinguists use these tools to study variable data, and how their methods can be applied to the study of interlanguage.

An example of a continuum that has been studied by sociolinguists is the style continuum. In informal speech, such as a conversation with friends, New Yorkers are likely to delete postvocalic /r/, pronouncing fourth floor /fɔəﬂɔə/. In formal speech, postvocalic /r/ is more likely to be present because (according to Labov 1972) these speakers desire to sound more correct. Figure 2.1 shows how /r/ deletion is affected by formal and informal speech style, and also by the speaker's social class. Lower middle class New Yorkers supply postvocalic /r/ about 8 percent of the time in casual style but more often in more formal styles. Formal speech styles can be elicited by giving the speaker tasks which allow her to focus on the form of language. As Figure 2.1 shows, reading a prose passage elicits a fairly formal style, in which lower middle class speakers supply constricted /r/ about 28 percent of the time. Reading a word list elicits a more formal style, and reading a list of minimal pairs (in New York City dialect) such as law, lore, elicits the most formal style with the highest percentage of constricted /r/. Thus, depending on the circumstances of speaking, New Yorkers 'style shift' along a continuum of formality.

Figure 2.1   Class stratification of /r/ in guard, car, beer, beard, etc. for native New York City adults.

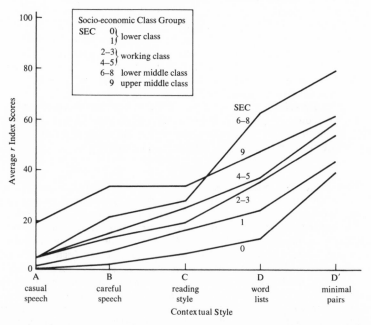

Figure 2.1 is an implicational hierarchy which displays not only the effect of the speaker's style on /r/ deletion, but also the effect of the speaker's socioeconomic class. It shows that upper middle class speak-

ers pronounce /r/ more often than middle class speakers, who pronounce it more often than lower class speakers, and so on. However,
notice that the difference in the speech of the various social classes is
not absolute. Lower class speakers use less /r/ less frequently than
upper middle class speakers in the same speech style, but upper middle
class speakers use /r/ less frequently in their casual speech than lower
class speakers do when they are reading word lists. Social dialects
within a speech community, then, differ not absolutely, but only with
regard to the frequency of variants. Thus, the speaking styles of all
social classes can be displayed on the same continuum.

Corder (1977) has pointed out that the continuum of social dialects
and speech styles in Figure 2.1 is different from the continua in interlanguages, which were discussed in Chapter 1. He calls a social dialect
continuum 'horizontal' since all social varieties are more or less equally
complex. An interlanguage continuum, on the other hand, is 'vertical'
since individual varieties range from simple to complex.

2. The wave model. A second tool that sociolinguists use to describe variation in adult native speaker speech is the 'wave model', a
kind of implicational hierarchy which shows how a linguistic change can
begin in one geographical area and spread to surrounding areas. To
take a hypothetical example, suppose that oil is discovered in a small
town in Utah and that a large refinery is built. Suppose that managers,
scientists, and technicians are brought in from the Midwest who intro-
duce midwestern speech patterns to the area. If these newcomers are
respected by the local residents, some Utahans will adopt features of
midwestern speech, and these features will gradually spread from the
town to the surrounding areas. This spread is described by the wave
model, as shown in Figure 2.2.

Figure 2.2   The wave model of the spread of a new speech form
through geographical space.

Time 0:	No new features.	
Time 1:	New feature a begins to appear in town.	a
Time 2:	Feature a spreads to area adjacent to town; new feature b begins to appear in town.	a, b a
Time 3:	Feature a spreads to more distant areas; feature b spreads to area adjacent to town; new feature c begins to appear in town.	a,b c a b a

It is important to note that when feature a begins to appear among
the Utahans who live in the town, it is not suddenly present in everyone's speech, nor even present all the time in the speech of an individual. Instead, the feature is variably present in the speech of any

particular Utahan. Thus, even at time 3, when feature b̲ has spread to the area adjacent to the town, feature a̲ will still be used only variably in the town. However, feature a̲ will be more frequent in the town than in the adjacent area. The diagram in time 3 of Figure 2.2 is an implicational hierarchy since feature c̲ implies the presence of features b̲ and a̲, and feature b̲ implies the presence of feature a̲.

A concrete example of the wave model can be found in Wolfram's (1969) study of Black English in Detroit. Wolfram looked at three socially stigmatized aspects of his subjects' speech: (1) the deletion of a final consonant in a consonant cluster; (2) the deletion of /r/ after a vowel; (3) /θ/ pronounced as /f/. Wolfram described these features of Black English (as I have just done) in terms of their contrast to the corresponding Standard English features. Such a comparison suggests that the speakers' internal representations of, for example, the word for 'light fog' is /mɪst/, not /mɪs/, and that the final /t/ is dropped because it is somewhat difficult to pronounce two consonants together (see Chapter 6, Section 2). However, to illustrate how the wave model works, it is more helpful to assume that at some point in its history Black English did not possess final consonant clusters (or postvocalic /r/ or /θ/) and that this Standard English feature has spread through the black speech community. Thus, the variation between Standard English and Black English forms is not caused by a rule which deletes the final consonant in a cluster, but by a rule which adds one. Wolfram's data show that in 1969 the three standard features CC#̸#̸, V /r/, and /θ/ were variably present in Detroit Black English. This information is contained in Figure 2.3.

Figure 2.3 Presence of Standard English features in Detroit Black speech.

Social class	θ replaces f	r in V_	cc#̸	Time (implied)
Lower class	.55	.29	.16	i
Lower working	.62	.39	.21	ii
Upper working	.89	.59	.34	iii
Upper middle	.94	.79	.49	iv

Notice that the three features can be implicationally ordered so that /θ/ is more frequent than V /r/, and that V /r/ is more frequent than CC#̸#̸. The features also stratify according to social class. As might be expected, all the standard features are more frequent in upper class speech than in lower class speech. The spread of a new linguistic form can be depicted by an implicational table which substitutes periods of time for social classes, as shown in the rightmost column of Figure 2.3. This substitution implies that historically /θ/ was the first of the three features to appear in Black English, followed by V /r/ and then by CC#̸#̸, and that the relative frequency of these rules has been maintained. Figure 2.3 also implies that the standard features originated in the speech of socially mobile speakers and spread to the working classes.

The wave model, then, shows how a linguistic feature can spread through geographical space, through social space, and through time. Thus, the hierarchical relationship among socioeconomic classes in

Figure 2.3 is the same as the hierarchical relationship among geographical areas in Figure 2.2. It is possible that other new features will
begin to appear in the speech of upper class Black English speakers and
spread to adjacent social classes just as features b and c spread in
Figure 2.2. It is likely that a new feature spreading from the upper
class will first appear in the formal style of a lower class speaker
since, in this style, speakers pay attention to or 'monitor'[1] the way they
talk.

3. Linguistic environment. We have considered how time,
geographhical space, social class and monitoring can affect the spread
of a new linguistic feature. Now consider the effect of a fifth factor--
linguistic environment. Fasold (1972) examined the effect of linguistic
environment on final stop deletion in the speech of working class blacks
in Washington, D.C. We have noted that at one time final consonant
clusters, including clusters ending in a stop, were apparently absent in
Black English and are now spreading; but for convenience most linguists
write a formal rule which implies that final clusters are represented in
the mental lexicons of speakers and are reduced through a phonological
rule. The present discussion reflects this approach. When the final
stop deletion rule studied by Fasold applies, mist is pronounced /mIs/
and wild is pronounced /wayl/. The frequency with which speakers
delete these final stops is influenced, or 'constrained', by the sounds
that precede and follow them. Thus, a following nonvowel (an obstru-
ent, liquid, or glide) favors deletion, and a preceding sonorant also
favors deletion.

Furthermore, the effect of the following nonvowel is stronger than
the effect of the preceding sonorant. The following nonvowel is therefore the stronger or 'first-order' constraint; the preceding sonorant is
the weaker or 'second-order' constraint. This situation can be illustrated in a 'cross-products' chart such as Figure 2.4. The linguistic
environment in which the most deletion occurs is where both the following nonvowel (first-order constraint) and the preceeding sonorant
(second-order constraint) are present, as in sand castle. The environment in which the least deletion occurs is where neither constraint is
present, as in lift it. When only one of the two constraints is present,
we can see which constraint is stronger since the stronger one will
cause more deletion. Examination of the data in Figure 2.4 shows that
when only the following nonvowel is present, the deletion rate is 68.8
percent; whereas when only the preceding sonorant is present, the
deletion rate is 34.9 percent. Thus, the following nonvowel is indeed
the stronger constraint.

Figure 2.4 shows that there are four linguistic environments in
which final stops can be deleted from a consonant cluster: (1) when the
first-order and second-order constraints are present; (2) when only the
first order constraint is present; (3) when only the second-order constraint is present; (4) when no constraints are present. Clearly, stop
deletion is most likely in environment (1) and least likely in environment (4).

4. Implicational tables. Sociolinguists have used implicational
hierarchies, in one form or another, to display the systematic effects
of socioeconomic class, the passage of time, monitoring, and linguistic

environment on the production of a linguistic feature. Language acquisition scholars have used implicational hierarchies to show the order of acquisition of linguistic features. In Chapter 1, it was suggested that this order is related to the complexity of the structures. In Chapter 2, five ways of displaying implicational relationships have been mentioned. These are: (1) a rank order, as in Dulay and Burt's morpheme studies; (2) a series of stages, as in Cazden et al.'s study of negative acquisition; (3) a graph, as in Labov's study of /r/ deletion in New York City; (4) a cross-products chart, as in Fasold's study of final consonant deletion in Black English; and (5) an implicational table, as in Wolfram's study of three Standard English features in Detroit Black English. The implicational table is the most widely used of these devices in sociolinguistic studies and, as will be seen in Chapter 3, it has replaced the rank order as the favored device in interlanguage studies. The implicational table is now considered in more detail.

Figure 2.4   A cross-products chart showing the correct ordering of constraints for final stop deletion in the speech of working-class blacks in Washington, D.C.

	Example:
	2nd-order constraint present (preceding sonorant) 83.3
	sand castle
1st-order constraint present (following nonvowel)	
	2nd order constraint absent (preceding obstruent) 68.8 **fast car**
	2nd-order constraint present (preceding sonorant) 34.9 **wild elephant**
1st-order constraint absent (following vowel)	
	2nd-order constraint absent (preceding obstruent) 25.2 **lift it**

An implicational table that we have already encountered is Figure 2.3, which shows the correlation of Standard English features with socioeconomic class in Detroit Black English. The cells in Figure 2.3 contain the percentages at which these features were supplied by the various classes. Comparing these percentages, one can see that / θ / is the most frequent feature for all classes, and that final consonant cluster is the least frequent feature for all classes. It would be possible to display just the information about the relative frequency of features without showing the actual percentages at which the features were supplied. To do this, we could convert the multivalued implicational table in Figure 2.3 into a two-valued implicational table, such as the one in Figure 2.5, in which the percentage figures are replaced by 1s and 0s. This replacement is done as follows: any percentage greater than 55 percent is replaced by a 1; any percentage less than or equal to 55 percent is replaced by a 0.

Figure 2.5   Figure 2.3 converted into a two-dimensional table.

Social class	θ replaces f	r in V_	cc#	Time (implied)
Lower class	0	0	0	i
Lower working	1	0	0	ii
Upper working	1	1	0	iii
Upper middle	1	1	0	iv

Notice that converting the multivalued implicational table in Figure 2.3 into the two-valued implicational table in Figure 2.5 obscures the difference between the linguistic variety spoken by the upper working class and the variety spoken by the upper middle class, so some important information is lost. Therefore, it is usually a bad idea to convert percentage data which pattern as nicely as the data in Figure 2.3 into a two-valued implicational table. However, it is often the case, especially in interlanguage studies, that the data do not pattern this nicely, and in these cases a two-valued implicational table can show patterns that would not be obvious in a multidimensional table. For example, what if, in Figure 2.3, the percentages for /θ/ and /r/ in the upper middle class were reversed, so that /θ/ was supplied at 79 percent and /r/ was supplied at 94 percent? This reversal would violate the pattern found in the other classes, but it would not imply that the relationship between the features and classes was entirely random. The reversal would mean that the use of Standard English features was more variable and less systematic, but there would still be some relationship. This weaker relationship could be displayed by means of the two-valued implicational table because both 94 percent application and 79 percent application would be translated into 1s. Thus, two-valued implicational tables do not make such strong claims as multivalued tables and are therefore suitable for displaying patterns in highly variable data.

Another possibility for displaying weak implicational relationships is a three-valued table such as Figure 2.6, which describes the effect of socioeconomic class and linguistic environment on a hypothetical rule. The rule modeled in Figure 2.6 has only one linguistic constraint, unlike the rule for final stop deletion, modeled in Figure 2.4, which has two constraints. In Figure 2.6, a 0 could be used to mean that the rule never applies, or that it applies at a low frequency, say less than ten percent; a 1 could mean that the rule always applies, or that it applies at a high frequency, say greater than 90 percent. An X would mean that the rule applies at a frequency between the frequencies designated by 0 and 1.

Figure 2.6   Hypothetical example of the influence of linguistic and socioeconomic class on a variable rule with one constraint.

Social class	Linguistic environment: Constraint absent	Constraint present
Highest	1	1
Upper middle	x	1
Lower middle	x	x
Upper working	0	⊃
Lower working	0	0

Key: 0 = categorical nonapplication of rule; x = variable application of rule; 1 = categorical application of rule.

A four-valued implicational table is illustrated in Section 5 of this chapter, which reviews a study of interlanguage phonology (which is usually more systematic than interlanguage syntax). In general, the more variable the data, the fewer the values that can be used in an implicational table for those data. Thus, the highly systematic relationship between socioeconomic class and the use of Standard English features in Detroit Black English allows the use of a table containing the actual percentage figures, as in Figure 2.3. On the other hand, the weakly systematic relationship between the use of target language features and language proficiency found in most interlanguage studies can be shown only in an implicational table containing four or fewer values.

5. The wave model in second language acquisition. This discussion shows that the wave model suggests the origins and the future direction of a linguistic change within a speech community. Perhaps the wave model can describe one way in which linguistic features spread in interlanguages as well. Gatbonton-Segalowitz (1976) tested this hypothesis in her cross-sectional study of how French Canadians acquire the English phoneme /ð/. She found that her subjects produced four phonetic versions of /ð/, namely: [ð, dð, d, θ]. English speaking informants to whom the subjects' tapes were played judged the first three of these variants to be native-like and the last one to be nonnativelike. Gatbonton-Segalowitz then considered how her subjects acquired a nativelike variant of /ð/. This acquisition can be described by rule (1).

Rule (1)

$$[\theta] \longrightarrow \left\{ \begin{array}{c} [ð] \\ [dð] \\ [d] \end{array} \right\}$$

Rule (1) says that [θ] , the nonnativelike variant, is replaced by one or more of the three nativelike variants as the speaker gains proficiency. Figure 2.7 shows the frequency with which 27 subjects applied rule (1). Two of the subjects always produced the nonnativelike variant. The other subjects had variable pronunciation, sometimes producing one of the nativelike variants and sometimes producing the nonnativelike variant.

Figure 2.7 Placement of Gatbonton-Segalowitz's subjects in the theoretical stages of phoneme acquisition.

Phase	Lect	Informants whose lects match the model's lects	Environmental categories EC1 EC2 EC3 EC4 EC5				
Acquisition	a	11,17	1	1	1	1	1
phase	b	1,10,12,14,15,16	1	1	1	1	12
	c	3,6,29	1	1	1	12	12
	d		1	1	12	12	12
	e		1	12	12	12	12
Transition	f	4	12	12	12	12	21
phase	g		12	12	12	21	21
	h		12	12	21	21	21
	i	24,25,28	12	21	21	21	21
	j		21	21	21	21	21
Replacement	k	14,22,27	21	21	21	21	2
phase	l	21	21	21	21	2	2
	m		21	21	2	2	2
	n		21	2	2	2	2
	o		2	2	2	2	2

Key: 1=all tokens judged 'nonnativelike'; 12=variable pronunciation, most tokens judged 'nonnativelike'; 21=variable pronunciation, most tokens judged 'nativelike'; 2=all tokens judged 'nativelike'.

Gatbonton-Segalowitz used a four-valued implicational table to describe the continuum of /ð/ acquisition. She defined the four values in the table as follows:

1   = all nonnativelike variants

1.2 = nonnativelike and nativelike variants,
        nonnativelike predominating

2:1 = nonnativelike and nativelike variants,
        nativelike predominating

2   = all nativelike variants

As noted above, for native speakers the linguistic environment influences the frequency with which a variant is supplied. Gatbonton-Segalowitz found environmental influences for nonnative speakers as well. Figure 2.7 displays all of the possible linguistic environments in which rule (1) can occur. Environmental category (EC) 5 is the 'heaviest' (most favorable) environment and EC 1 is the 'lightest' (least favorable) environment. If rule (1) were to describe a linguistic change moving through a speech community, the wave model predicts that the rule would begin to apply, variably, in the heaviest environment. The rule would then spread, variably, to the second heaviest environment, while applying at a higher frequency in the heaviest environment. Gatbonton-Segalowitz asked whether this mechanism of language change works when a rule is acquired by an individual learner. The array of 1s and 2s in Figure 2.7 contains all of the stages consistent with the wave model for the spread of rule (1). The first part of the table, the acquisition phase, shows the theoretical stages in which rule (1) goes from categorical nonapplication to variable application (with the nonnativelike form more frequent) in all environments. The middle part of Figure 2.7, the transition phase, shows the theoretical stages in which the rule changes from less than 50 percent application. The last part of Figure 2.7, the replacement phase, shows the theoretical stages through which the rule passes as it moves from greater than fifty percent application to categorical application. Gatbonton-Segalowitz then asked how many of these theoretical stages (or 'lects') were represented in the speech of her subjects. The rightmost column of Figure 2.7 shows which subjects are at a particular stage. Of the 27 subjects, 19 fit the theoretical model. The other 8 subjects apply rule (1) more frequently in a lighter environment than in a heavier one, and therefore do not fit the implicational hierarchy.

Gatbonton-Segalowitz's study did not prove conclusively that second language learners acquire a rule in the same way in which a rule spreads through the speech community, since only 70 percent of her subjects fit the pattern consistent with the wave model and since her study was cross-sectional and not longitudinal. Nevertheless, she demonstrated that the speech of the majority of her subjects could be described by means of an implicational hierarchy, and thus that developmental continua can be found in interlanguage data.

6. **Variable rules.** The discussion so far has shown that certain rules apply more often in some linguistic environments than in others, and that environmental factors which favor the application of a rule are called constraints. Since traditional transformational-generative (T-G) rules do not specify constraints on a rule, variationists have developed a new kind of rule, called a 'variable rule'. Variable rules are written in T-G notation, but are conceptually very different from Chomskyan rules. T-G rules are of two kinds: obligatory and optional. An optional rule relates two forms which 'mean the same thing'. It could be used to describe final stop deletion in Black English since sometimes speakers pronounce these stops and sometimes they don't, and since deleting the final stop does not change the meaning of the word in context. But a variable rule is more precise than an optional rule: it specifies the linguistic environments in which stop deletion is more likely to occur.

Generative grammarians have not rushed to exchange optional rules for the more precise variable rules. Kay (1978) points out that this reluctance is consistent with the T-G model of grammar, which is designed to specify which forms a language allows and which forms it doesn't allow, not how often forms occur. Such a grammar describes an idealized and abstract system and so is of limited use to linguists who study performance data. Chapter 5 considers in detail the relationship between the abstract approach to linguistics and the data oriented approach, but for now we note that variable rules can describe the way speakers use language more accurately than optional rules.

Variable rules were developed to describe aspects of nonstandard English, such as final consonant deletion, but they can be used to describe aspects of interlanguage as well. For example, Gatbonton-Segalowitz could have used a variable rule to describe the acquisition of /ð/ by French Canadians. To write this rule, one would have to specify the linguistic constraints which combine to make up the five possible environments, EC 1-5. Since these constraints are somewhat complicated, a different example of a variable rule in interlanguage is considered, a rule used by Hyltenstam (1977) to describe sentential negation by adults acquiring Swedish.

Hyltenstam looked at how learners from a number of different language backgrounds acquired the Swedish negative particle inte. He found that in the first stage of the acquisition of sentential negatives, learners always placed inte before the finite verb in both main and subordinate clauses. In the final stage learners correctly placed inte after the finite verb in main clauses and before the finite verb in subordinate clauses. Hyltenstam described the second stage of negative acquisition with rule (2a).

Rule (2a) Variable Neg particle movement.

$$\left[X - Neg - \left\{ \begin{array}{c} Aux_{fin} \\ MV_{fin} \end{array} \right\} - Y \right]_S$$

SD:	1	(2)	3		4 $\Longrightarrow$
SC:	1		3	(2)	4

3:	Aux_{fin}	MV_{fin}
order	alpha	beta

Rule (2a) says that inte is sometimes moved from before the verb to after the verb, and that the nature of the verb determines how often this movement occurs. If the finite verb is an auxiliary verb, rule (2a) is more likely to apply than if the finite verb is a main verb. In other words, Aux_{fin} is a heavier environment for the Neg Movement Rule than MV_{fin}. In rule (2a) the constraints do not combine to produce several linguistic environments, as they did in Figure 2.4. This is because in rule (2a) the constraints are mutually exclusive: each constraint specifies a different type of verb. The relative strength of the two constraints is given in the small table which accompanies rule (2a), where Aux_{fin} is identified as the first-order or 'alpha constraint', and MV_{fin} as the second-order or 'beta constraint'.

Hyltenstam's use of tables to specify the relative strength of the constraints is not the only way of presenting this information. Some linguists prefer to insert the alpha and beta notation directly into the rule in front of the constraints to which these symbols apply. This method is shown in rule (2b), which is a different way of writing rule rule (2a).

Rule (2b) A different way of writing rule (2a).

$$\left[X - Neg - \left\{ \begin{array}{c} A\ (Aux_{fin}) \\ B\ (MV_{fin}) \end{array} \right\} - Y \right]_S$$

$$
\begin{array}{ccccc}
1 & (2) & 3 & & 4 \implies \\
1 & & 3 & (2) & 4
\end{array}
$$

Like an implicational table, rule (2)--both (2a) and (2b)--predicts all of the theoretical stages for acquiring the Neg Movement transformation. Figure 2.8 converts the information contained in rule (2) into an implicational hierarchy whose dimensions are time and linguistic environment. Thus, Figure 2.8 shows how rule (2) could spread and become a categorical rule. The rightmost column of Figure 2.8 contains a linguistic rule which describes the speech of subjects at each stage of acquisition.

Figure 2.8   Implicational hierarchy showing the spread of rule (2).

Time	Environments Light MVfin	Heavy AUXfin	Linguistic rule which describes this stage
1	0	0	N1 X - NEG - Vfin - Y
2	0	x	N2 X - NEG - AUXfin - Y
			1 (2) 3 4⟹1 3 (2) 4
3	x	x	Rule (2)
4	x	1	N3 X - NEG - MVfin - Y
			*AUXfin
			1 (2) 3 4⟹1 3 (2) 4
5	1	1	N4 X - Vfin - NEG - Y

Key: 0=categorical application of rule (2); x=variable application of rule (2); 1=categorical nonapplication of rule (2); Vfin=finite verb (either auxiliary or main verb); AUXfin=finite auxiliary verb; MVfin=finite main verb.

According to Figure 2.8, at time 1 a subject always places the Neg particle <u>inte</u> before the finite verb. This fact can be described with phrase structure rule N1; no Neg Movement rule is necessary. At time 2, the learner begins to move the Neg particle variably in the heavier linguistic environment. The rule which describes this stage, N2, says that Neg Movement sometimes occurs when the finite verb is an auxiliary. At time 3, movement of the Neg particle occurs variably with both auxiliary and main verbs, but more frequently with auxiliary verbs. To describe this stage, we employ variable rule (2), which specifies the relative strengths of the two linguistic environments. At time 4, movement of the Neg particle still occurs variably when the finite verb is a main verb, but now it always occurs when the finite verb is an auxiliary. This categorical application in the heavy environment is shown in rule N3 by placing an asterisk before Aux_{fin}. The asterisk indicates that Aux_{fin} is a 'knockout constraint', whose presence guarantees the application of the rule. Finally, at time 5, the Neg

Movement Rule applies categorically, since the learner always places inte after the verb. This fact is described by rule N4, a phrase structure rule. At this point, the learner's internal rule has been completely restructured, as can be seen by comparing rule N1 with rule N4.

According to Hyltenstam, as the learner progresses to the final stage of sentential negative formation, she must develop a variable rule that moves the Neg particle back before the finite verb when the verb occurs in a subordinate clause. Thus, the complete restructuring of the learner's grammar represented by the replacement of N1 by N4 probably never occurs for most speakers, since their internal grammars must continue to change with regard to the placement of the Neg particle. But let us suppose that rule N4 represents the target stage, so that we may consider whether second language acquisition is best described by categorical rules such as rule N4 or by variable rules such as rule (2). Rule N4 implies that the learner never reverts to the old habit of placing Neg before the verb. But language teachers know that most learners backslide, at least sometimes. If a learner ever produces a form found in stages 1 through 4, she exhibits variable performance, and a categorical rule, such as N4, is not appropriate.

The phenomenon of backsliding, then, suggests that rule (2) best describes most learners' speech. The frequency of application of this rule may become very high in both heavy and light environments, but rule (2) predicts that there will be occasional backsliding. The rule also predicts the linguistic environment in which backsliding is most likely to occur, namely, the light environment.

Hyltenstam concluded that his subjects followed a very regular path in the acquisition of the Swedish negative, and that this path could be modeled by a variable rule.

Note

1. Labov uses the word monitor differently than Krashen (1982) does. The difference between Labov's and Krashen's theories of monitoring are discussed in Chapter 8.

Chapter 3

PIDGINS, CREOLES, AND INTERLANGUAGES

1. **Pidgins and creoles.** In Chapter 2 we saw that not everyone in a speech community speaks exactly alike, but that the variation is not random. The speech of individuals and groups, such as social classes, can be placed along a continuum in which the linguistic environment and monitoring will affect most individuals' application of a rule in the same way. Continua are found where a linguistic change is taking place, as in the case of /r/ deletion in New York City. Speakers at one end of the continuum are the forerunners of an ongoing change, while speakers at the other end are as yet relatively unaffected by the change. Now consider two other types of speech communities where linguistic continua are found: pidgin- and creole-speaking communities. A number of scholars have noticed the similarities among pidgins, creoles, and interlanguages.

Linguists have disagreed about the definitions of pidgin language and creole language. The traditional distinction is based on how the two varieties come into being. 'Pidgins' are created when speakers of two different languages come into contact, as when slaves are forcibly relocated, or when trade develops between two groups. In these circumstances, people must develop a lingua franca in which to communicate. What results is a pidgin--an invented second language. A creole, on the other hand, is an invented first language. It is created when members of the two language groups which developed the pidgin intermarry and have children. These children will learn the pidgin as their first language. However, since a pidgin is not as complex as a standard language and does not fill all the needs of human communication, the children will expand and elaborate it, adding such things as articles and aspect markers. The resulting language is a 'creole'.

Ferguson and DeBose (1977) claim that this traditional distinction between pidgins and creoles, which is based on origins, is not adequate, and that we must also make a distinction, based on complexity, between very simple pidgins (sometimes called prepidgins or jargons) and more complex pidgins. They note that many pidgins, such as West African Pidgin English, Tok Pisin, and Sango, are as stable, complex, and autonomous as creoles, and therefore they exclude these mature varieties of contact languages from their definition of pidgin. Accord-

ing to Ferguson and DeBose, true pidgins arise when a speaker of a
primary language P attempts to learn second language S but is not
entirely successful. The unsuccessful learner produces a variety of S
which is reduced and simplified and which has the phonological and
morphosyntactic characteristics of P. This process of simplification is
called 'pidginization'. Schumann (1978) lists the following characteristics of simplification in pidgin languages: (1) Articles are usually
missing. (2) Possession is indicated by simple juxtaposition: 'white man
mouth.' (3) Inflectional features are lost; the simple form of the verb
is used exclusively. (4) Verbs are negated by using no: 'he no run
away.' In Ferguson and DeBose's account, then, true pidgin languages
and the less advanced forms of interlanguages are similar, because both
contain structures transferred from P and simplified structures from S.

Ferguson and DeBose believe that pidginization alone is not sufficient to produce a pidgin language, even in their restricted sense of the
term. After pidginization has occurred, the pidginized variety must be
somewhat expanded and elaborated, so that it can be used in a wide
range of communicative contexts. This elaboration is called 'depidginization', and it usually occurs in a pidgin-speaking community over
several generations. Different pidgins show different degrees of elaboration. For example, Tay Boi is more depidginized that Chinook
Jargon. Late in the depidginization process, a contact language becomes as elaborate as a creole or a standard language, as is the case
with Tok Pisin and West African Pidgin English, and therefore, according to Ferguson and DeBose, the contact language ceases to be a true
pidgin.

2. Bickerton's theory of pidginization. Bickerton (1981) has a very
different view of pidginization, but he, too, makes a distinction between incipient and mature pidgin languages. Hawaiian Pidgin English
(HPE) is a true pidgin because it was quickly replaced by a creole and
therefore did not have time to depidginize. Tok Pisin, on the other
hand, did depidginize. In the past, Papua/New Guinean children used
Tok Pisin only as a second language, preserving their parents' language
as their first. Only now, after several generations, is Tok Pisin beginning to acquire native speakers. Although Ferguson and DeBose see
little difference between mature pidgins and creoles (since both are
equally complex), Bickerton sees a great difference. In Bickerton's
account, creoles are created by children who grow up surrounded by an
impoverished language—namely, a pidgin. These children learn the
pidgin as their first language, but since it is not adequate for all their
communicative needs, the children expand and elaborate the pidgin,
adding articles, possessive markers, inflections, and other features.
Where do these new features come from? According to Bickerton, they
come from the children's minds—from their innate linguistic knowledge. Thus, creoles are rich in linguistic and cognitive universals and
their study can shed light on how the mind works. Bickerton's account
of creolization is discussed more fully in Chapter 4; but now consider
his account of pidginization, which he claims is an entirely different
process.

Bickerton emphasizes the role of transfer in pidginization, noting,
for example, that Japanese speakers of HPE usually use the subject-

verb order of Japanese, whereas Filipino speakers usually use the verb-subject order of their native language (most often Illocano). Similarly, Japanese speakers often express <u>when</u> clauses with compound nominals, as in Japanese:

as-bihoa-stei-taim
us-before-stay-time
'when we used to live here' (Bickerton 1981:12)

But Filipino speakers, whose languages do not contain these structures, seldom use them. Thus, Bickerton sees pidginization as the relexification of the speaker's native language. He has claimed that the same process is involved in second language acquisition:

Pidginization is second language learning with restricted input (1977:49).

Scanty evidence ... does indicate that second languages are naturally acquired via piecemeal relexification, productive calquing and the utilization of mother-tongue surface syntax (much as in the case of Hawaiian Pidgin English) (1977:55).

3. Universals in pidginization. According to Anderson (1983:30): 'Bickerton's relexification view of pidginization excludes any possible role for universals.' However, other linguists believe that language universals are involved in linguistic simplification. In Chapter 1, we saw that notions of simplicity are important to theories of first language acquisition. Thus, Brown explained similar morpheme acquisition orders by saying that certain morphemes are syntactically and semantically simpler in a universal sense, and Traugott claimed that there is a natural semantax, or universally simple code. Among the first scholars to propose that language universals are involved in pidginization were Kay and Sankoff (1974), who claimed that this involvement could occur in two ways. Suppose P and S use different surface structures to express the same semantic structure, and suppose that P's structure is universally simpler than S's structure. A hypothetical example would be tag questions, which are very complex in English but very simple in Amharic, consisting of the single word /aydellum/. It is likely that an Amharic/English pidgin would adopt the Amharic way of making tag questions. On the other hand, the pidgin might adopt English-like verb tenses, since these are simpler in English than in Amharic. For example, in the simple present tense the Amharic verb has 11 forms, the English verb only two. An Amharic/English pidgin, then, would be simpler than either parent language since it would incorporate the simplest patterns of both.

Language universals might also bring about simplification when P and S share certain surface structures. If this is so, it will be easy for speakers of P to learn the equivalent structures in S. Kay and Sankoff (1974:67-68) note:

Indeed these shared structures will be the first and perhaps the only structures that speaker-hearers learn to produce and interpret correctly in the other's language. These constructions then form the natural grammatical basis for a pidgin.

Corder (1981) suggests a provocative explanation of simplification in second language acquisition (SLA) which incorporates both Traugott's idea of natural semantax and Bickerton's idea of relexification. First of all, Corder claims that simplification is not an appropriate term for the first step in SLA because it implies that the learner controls the target language but chooses to use only certain of its structures. Parents simplify in this sense when they speak 'motherese' to their children, as do teachers when they speak 'teacher talk' to their students. These varieties have short sentences, concrete referents, and careful pronunciation. According to Corder, a second language learner cannot simplify the target language in this sense because she does not possess it. Nor does the second language learner directly access language universals, as the child may access natural semantax. Rather, the learner simplifies the native language by using her knowledge of natural semantax, as she does in speaking motherese, and then relexifies this simple code with forms from the target language.

> If simplification plays any part in second language acquisition as a process or learning strategy, then it is not the target language system which is being simplified but that of the mother tongue, i.e., that which is already known; and the simplification is toward some basic universal language--natural semantax, which represents the starting point for second language acquisition (Corder 1981:151).

So, according to Corder, SLA is not exactly like first language acquisition since in the latter case universals are directly tapped, while in the former they are 'remembered', or accessed via the first language.

Meisel (1983), disagreeing with both Bickerton and Corder, claims that second language learners may very well base their hypotheses about how the target language works directly on language universals, as first language learners do. If this is so, 'simplification', correctly describes the mental process that results in interlanguage. It is not necessary for learners to simplify and then relexify their language any more than it is necessary for children to do this.

> Language acquisition is ... the learner's forming hypotheses about the structure of the target language. This activity ... is structured by perceptual and   expressive strategies. In other words there is something happening ontogenetically even if the learner does not have available the more complex variety (Meisel 1983:127).

As an example of a universal expressive strategy in second language acquisition, Meisel points to a widespread way of negating main verbs. In the incipient pidgin language of Japanese bargirls and American servicemen, <u>not</u> is inserted immediately before the negated predicate, unlike either Japanese or English. According to Bickerton (cited in Meisel 1983:55), this pattern is also found in most pidgins and creoles.

Meisel found that Spanish, Italian, and Portugese speakers acquiring German also placed the negative marker directly before or after the main verb, even though correct German requires the marker at the end of the clause. Thus, these speakers produced sentences like (1) instead of sentences like (2).

(1) Ich $\begin{Bmatrix} \text{nicht} \\ \text{kein} \end{Bmatrix}$ rauche beim Essen.

     I   Neg   smoke   during dinner

(2) Ich rauche beim   Essen   nicht.

     I   smoke   during dinner Neg

In fact, Meisel found that his subjects almost never placed Neg in correct clause-final position. 'This is noteworthy since with most other word order problems ... there is usually a lot of variation in the probability of use of standard forms' (Meisel 1983:133). Of course, Neg is placed before the main verb in the Romance languages of the subjects, but Meisel showed that transfer cannot explain their performance. A transfer explanation predicts that Neg will also be found before Aux, modal, and copula, since Romance languages place Neg before all finite verbs. However, the Neg + Modal + Verb sequence occurs just once in Meisel's data, whereas there are numerous examples of Neg placed after modals, Auxs, and copulas, and before the main verb.

Meisel (1981:134) postulates a universal strategy for Neg placement: 'Place Neg immediately before the constituent to be negated.' This strategy is consistent with Slobin's (1973:199) operating principle: 'avoid interruption or rearrangement of linguistic units.' German negation requires speakers to rearrange words which logically function as a unit, so it is difficult in a language universal sense and therefore is acquired late.

4. The nativization hypothesis. Anderson (1983) proposes a comprehensive theory to explain the similarities of pidgins, creoles, and interlanguages. His 'nativization hypothesis' claims that language universals are found in all three varieties. With Bickerton, he observes that creoles contain many features not present in the parent pidgins which reflect linguistic universals such as Traugott's natural semantax, Slobin's operating principles and, perhaps, Bickerton's cognitive universals, to be discussed in Chapter 4. Thus, in their initial stages, creoles develop in the direction of internal consistency and universal simplicity, both of which reflect norms internal to their speakers rather than norms which already exist in a speech community. 'Nativization' is movement in the direction of such internal norms. Nativization also occurs in the creation of pidgins and interlanguages, but in these cases the learner's internal norm is determined by the native language as well as by universals. In the initial stages, pidgin speakers and interlanguage speakers transfer structures from their native languages and also access universals.

'Denativization' results when a speaker of an individual nativized variety is exposed to more input from a standard language. When such input is available, the simplified variety expands by incorporating structures from the standard language. In the case of pidgins and creoles, this contact creates a continuum where speakers who have little contact with the standard language speak a nativized variety called the 'basilect', speakers who have more contact speak a partially denativized variety called the 'mesolect', and speakers who have the most contact speak a variety very similar to the standard language called the 'acrolect'. The denativization of a pidgin, then, is what Ferguson and DeBose called depidginization. The denativization of a creole is called 'decreolization'. Anderson's hypothesis builds on the work of Schumann (1978) and Stauble (1978), who drew the parallel between pidgin/creole continua and interlanguage continua, labeling the various interlanguage stages 'basilang', 'mesolang', and 'acrolang'.

As an example of a continuum in a pidgin language, Anderson (1981) cites Bickerton and Odo's (1976) study of negation in HPE, as displayed in Figure 3.1a.

Figure 3.1a   The continuum of negative structures in Hawaiian Pidgin English. For examples, see Figure 3.1b.

Lect	Speaker	$\%no^1$ etc.	$na(t)$	neva	kaenat	don^2	negAux^3
I	FF74K	100.0	-	-	-	-	-
	FJ66K	100.0	-	-	-	-	-
	MJ92H	94.7	-	2	-	-	-
	MF70H	94.6	-	2	-	-	-
II	MF71H	96.4	1	-	1	-	-
	MF69H	94.0	3	-	-	-	-
	MJ66H	89.4	7	-	-	-	-
	FJ70K	84.6	6	-	-	-	-
	MF75M	86.6	2	-	3	-	-
	FJ59H	81.0	7	-	-	1	-
	MF73K	73.7	9	-	-	1	-
III	MF77H	94.9	11	2	-	-	-
	FK79O	86.2	2	2	-	-	-
	MF85O	84.2	2	5	-	-	-
	MF74)	84.0	3	4	-	2	-
	FJ60K	76.7	9	5	-	-	-
IV	MF64K	90.2	3	1	1	-	-
	MF64M	86.1	2	4	5	-	-
	MJ77K	56.5	5	6	9	-	-
*V	FF70H	70.9	19	2	6	1	-
*	MF65O	62.8	10	-	2	4	-
*	MF67O	54.0	16	10	1	3	-
VI	MF64Oa	52.7	5	1	4	5	1
	MF64Ob	43.4	24	14	40	8	6
	Total		146	60	72	25	7

* = Alberto

[1] includes *no, no kaen, no mo.*

[2] except *dono*

[3] sandhi forms of negative + copular, negative + modal etc.

Basilect speaker FF74K negates in an extremely simple way: by putting no in front of the verb. But on the other end of the continuum, speaker MF64OB variably uses more standard-like forms, including kaenat and don. Notice that the HPE continuum shows much more variation than the American English social dialect continuum, where speakers in the lower socioeconomic classes might negate present tense main verbs using only two variants: <u>don't</u> and <u>doesn't</u>. But HPE speaker MF64Ob negates main verbs (excluding the negated Aux <u>kaenot</u>) in no less than five different ways.

Figure 3.1b   Examples of the negative structures in Figure 3.1a.

TYPE	EXAMPLE NUMBER	SPEAKER NUMBER	EXAMPLE
no V	3.210	MF77H	yu no go hom pilipin ailen? "Didn't you go home to the Philippines?"
no moa	3.214	FJ66K	nau no mo friza, "Now I haven't got a refrigerator."
no kaen	3.212	FF74K	no ken ispik inglis, "I can't speak English."
nat	3.217	MF75M	nat tu mach dipren bisayan aen tagalog, "Bisayan and Tagalog aren't very different."
neva	3.224	MF67O	ai neva go da taim, "I didn't go then."
kaenat	3.228	MF75M	bat mos mi, ai kaenat tawk tagalog, "But for the most part, as for me, I can't speak very much Tagalog."
don	3.232	MF64Ob	sam da ada feirans, dei don advaiz gud da silren, "Some other parents don't give their children good advice."
negAux	no examples given		

Anderson illustrates the similarity of pidgins and interlanguages by placing Schumann's subject Alberto, an adult Spanish speaker acquiring English, on the pidgin continuum of Figure 3.1a, where he would (more or less) fit in lect V, as indicated by the asterisks. Notice that although Alberto's English has fossilized at an elementary level, he still ranks fairly high on the continuum.

5. An invariant continuum. Pidgins, creoles, and interlanguages have been discussed from a language universals perspective, suggesting that in these varieties there is an implicational hierarchy of structures through which most acquirers pass, and that this hierarchy is motivated by semantic and syntactic complexity. However, the order in which different structures are acquired is not invariant. It appears to be the most probable order, but there are plenty of exceptions. The greatest amount of individual variation is found in the acquisition of morphemes, as Anderson (1977) has pointed out. The morpheme studies compare unrelated structures, such as articles and verb inflections. More regularity is found in the studies of a single subsystem, such as Schumann's study of English negation and Hyltenstam's study of Swedish negation. One such study has discovered an invariant order of acquisition, and this important study is considered next.

The ZISA (Zweitspracherwerb italienischer und spanischer Arbeiter) group conducted a cross-sectional study of 45 immigrant workers from Spain, Portugal, and Italy who were acquiring German naturalistically (Meisel 1983; Meisel, Clahsen, and Pienemann, 1981). They found that all their subjects began with the basic word order SVO (with the possibility of deletions). This order must be changed in Standard German in clauses involving adverbs, auxiliary verbs, and particles. These permutations are accomplished by means of three movement transfor-

mations: (1) Adverb Preposing, (2) Verb Separation (SEP), which is
illustrated in Figure 3.2, and (3) Subject-Verb Inversion.

Figure 3.2   Examples of SEP movement transformation.

Environments for SEP	Input	Output
1. Modal and Main Verb	Ich will kaufen dieses Buch. I want to buy this book.	Ich will dieses Buch kaufen.
2. Aux and Past Participle	Ich habe gebaut ein Haus. I have bought a house.	Ich habe ein Haus gebaut.
3. Particle and Verb	Fritz schaut an das Bild. Fritz looks at the picture.	Fritz schaut das Bild an.
4. Complex verb group including Particle	Ich habe geschaut an ein Haus. I have looked at a house.	Ich habe ein Haus angeschaut.

The transformations are implicationally related so that:

(3) ---➤ (2) ---➤ (1)

Before discussing why the transformations are ordered in this way, we
consider how the SEP movement rule emerged. In particular, consider
whether the ZISA group's data support the wave model prediction that
new rules begin in a particular environment and then spread to other
environments and, if this prediction is correct, whether these environments are ordered in the same way for all speakers. Figure 3.3 shows
how six of the ZISA subjects acquired the SEP rule.

Figure 3.3   Environments in which six learners acquired the SEP
movement transformation.

Environments for SEP	Learners: Janni	Benito	Maria	Franco	Angelina	Lolita
All environs.	1.	0.82	0.93	0.58	0.71	0.57
Environ. 1	1.	0.77	1.	...	...	0.67
Environ. 2	1.	0.71	1.	0.59	0.7	0.5
Environ. 3	1.	1.	...	...	...	...
Environ. 4	1.	1.	0.67	...	...	...

See Figure 3.2 for examples of Environments 1-4.

Apparently, the first stage in acquiring SEP (which is not shown in
Figure 3.3) is the same for all subjects: canonical word order is
preserved and SEP never applies. This fact supports the nativization
hypothesis claim that acquirers' first utterances are universally simple
forms. Sentences without SEP are simpler because SEP breaks up
elements which conceptually go together.

When the ZISA group's subjects began to use SEP, they did not all begin to use it in the same environment. It was not the case that all the subjects first began to apply SEP in, say, the environment Modal + Verb, and then moved on to Aux and Past Participle, and so on. In Figure 3.3, there are three cases where one can check to see whether the environments are ordered in the same way for all speakers. In two of the three test cases, Lolita and Maria, the environments are ordered in the same way since environment 1 is the lightest environment and environment 4 is the heaviest. However, Benito's data pattern differently. He applies SEP 100% in environment 4 and 100% in environment 1. These admittedly limited data suggest that the wave model prediction may hold for individual acquirers: rule acquisition may begin in one environment and spread to other environments. But the prediction that all the environments are similarly ordered is not supported here. It might still be the case that the environments are similarly ordered for most speakers, but it is impossible to determine whether this is so with the limited data available.

We now return to the question of why the subjects first acquired Adverb Preposing, then SEP, and finally Subject-Verb Inversion. The ZISA group explains this ordering on the basis of cognitive complexity. Adverb Fronting is the least complex of the three transformations because an adverb is a relatively independent element. Conceptually, it is not as important to a clause as the subject or the direct object. Furthermore, Adverb Fronting moves an element from sentence final to sentence initial--two salient positions. SEP is more complex than Adverb Fronting because it rearranges closely connected elements, namely Aux and past participle, and therefore violates Slobin's operating principle (1973:199) already mentioned, 'avoid interruption or rearrangement of linguistic units'. Subject-Verb Inversion is more complex than Adverb Fronting because it applies to sentences that already have a fronted adverb. Similarly, Subject-Verb Inversion is more complex than SEP because it applies to sentences that already have a separated verb.

In one respect, the ZISA group's findings are like the findings by Brown (1973), Dulay and Burt (1974), and Cazden et al. (1975), discussed in Chapter 1, since all of these researchers discovered implicational hierarchies in the acquisition of structures. Yet in another respect, the findings are very different. The ZISA group discovered an invariant hierarchy while the other researchers discovered only a statistically probably hierarchy. How can this difference be explained? One explanation was mentioned at the beginning of this section: the ZISA group studied the closely related structures of a linguistic subsystem, whereas Brown and Dulay and Burt studied unrelated structures such as articles and verb inflections. A second explanation is that some of the German word order transformations are logically prior to others. As we have seen, both Adverb Fronting and SEP serve as input to Subject-Verb Inversion, so they must be learned first.

A similar phenomenon was discovered by Cazden and Brown (1975), who found that their subjects acquired tag questions after they had acquired pronouns. They explained this order of acquisition on the basis of cognitive complexity. Tag Question Formation is more complex than Pronominalization since Pronominalization plus other things are required for Tag Question Formation. The invariant order of

German word order acquisition found by the ZISA group can be mostly explained by similar reasoning.

In addition to studying the acquisition of word order rules, the ZISA group looked at some of the morphemes studies by previous researchers, such as the copula. They found considerable individual variation in copula acquisition. Pienemann (1984:7) notes: 'There are correct copula structures at early stages with some learners, and with other learners the copula may be omitted even at advanced stages.'

The ZISA group proposes that since the continuum of word order rules is the same for all learners, it forms a kind of skeleton on which the flesh of other rules, such as Copula Insertion, can hang in various ways (although it seems likely that these other rules are implicationally related in a looser, statistical sense). Some speakers might acquire Copula Insertion before Adverb Fronting, others after SEP, and so. The ZISA group has attempted to explain this variation among individuals in terms of two different expressive strategies that an acquirer might adopt. One strategy is 'restrictive simplification', 'which is applied to minimize processing efforts when using the foreign language' (Meisel, Clahsen, and Pienemann 1981:121). A speaker using restrictive simplification might, for example, be able to prepose the adverb of a sentence, but at the expense of deleting the copula. Meisel (1983) calls this an 'effective' strategy, since the preposed adverb might be the sentence topic and therefore important, whereas the copula would probably be redundant. Speakers who often use restrictive simplification sacrifice accuracy for communicative efficiency. They might move fairly far along the word order continuum, but their speech would still be pidginized because they would often omit copulas, articles, and inflections. The concept of restrictive simplification implies that the interlanguage continuum is multidimensional. The vertical dimension of the continuum contains stages of increasing complexity defined by word order rules; the horizontal dimension allows for individual variation in acquiring 'soft tissue' structures like copulas and articles.

Notice, however, that the notion of restrictive simplification suggests that, in a sense, there may be less individual variation in the order of morpheme learning than is currently supposed. Perhaps some of the variability in the discovered orders may be caused by restrictive simplification. This is so because speakers may internalize a mental representation of morphemes in a fairly regular order, but this regularity may not be apparent in their speech since they delete many morphemes by restrictive simplification.

6. Linguistic variables and social variables. Variationist approaches to language have always emphasized the relationship of social and cultural factors to language variety. An example of how affective factors influence native speaker speech is found in Labov's (1972) study of diphthong centralization on Martha's Vineyard. Centralization causes /aw/ to become /ə w/, so that about the house is pronounced aboot the hoose. Labov discovered that for the youngest generation of speakers, centralization correlated closely with social attitudes. Young men and women who chose to remain on Martha's Vineyard rather than to pursue greater economic opportunities elsewhere affirmed their identity as Vineyarders by reviving the traditional central-ized pronunciation, which had almost died out.

During the 1970s, sociolinguists argued about whether social factors should be written into variable rules. For example, as we have seen, a speaker's social class correlates strongly with the speaker's frequency of final consonant deletion. Should social class be considered a con-straint on final consonant deletion just like a following vowel? The general consensus was that only linguistic factors have psychological status and should, therefore, be written into variable rules. Social factors were considered 'determining factors' which set limits within which linguistic constraints and monitoring could operate.

An example of the correlation between social factors and interlan-guage variety comes from Gatbonton-Segalowitz's (1976) study of French Canadians acquiring English, discussed in Chapter 2. Gatbonton-Segalowitz found that acquisition of /ð/ correlated with her subjects' political opinions. Subjects who favored the separation of Quebec from the rest of Canada placed lower on the continuum of /ð/ acquisition than subjects who did not favor separation. This finding does not imply that the former group did not achieve a high proficiency in English, only that they retained a French accent.

Schumann's (1978, 1983, 1984) 'acculturation hypothesis' is the most ambitious attempt to link social and psychological factors with inter-language variety. The hypothesis makes three claims about untutored second language acquisition. The first claim is that the earliest stage of interlanguage is reduced and simplified. The evidence supporting this claim, which was originally called the 'pidginization hypothesis', was discussed in Sections 3 and 4. Notice that Anderson's nativization hypothesis is basically an extension of Schumann's original insight. Schumann's second claim is that in the intermediate (mesolang) and final (acrolang) stages of second language acquisition there is a single continuum of structures which are acquired in the same order by all learners, and that the only kind of individual variation is the extent of learners' progress along this continuum before their interlanguage fossilizes. The ZISA group's research shows that this claim is wrong--the interlanguage continuum is (at least) bidimensional.

Schumann's third claim (1978:29) is that social and psychological factors determine a learner's ultimate proficiency in the second lan-guage:

> I would like to argue that two groups of variables--social fac-tors and affective factors--cluster into a single variable which is the major causal variable in SLA. I propose that we call this variable acculturation, ... the social and psychological inte-gration of the learner with the target language group.

Schumann found evidence for the acculturation hypothesis in his fa-mous study of Alberto, a 33-year-old Costa Rican, who immigrated to Cambridge, Massachusetts but did not acquire proficient English in spite of living in an English-speaking community. Schumann believes that Alberto's English fossilized because he did not desire to accultu-rate to American society. Like pidgin speakers, Alberto was isolated from the target language community, but for psychological and social, not physical, reasons.

Schmidt (1980) provides evidence against the acculturation hypothesis in his case study of Wes. Wes was a highly successful artist, 33 years old, who emigrated from Japan to Hawaii, where he developed extensive social and professional contacts in the English-speaking community. Thus, according to the acculturation hypothesis, Wes should be an excellent candidate to acquire proficient English. In fact, however, Wes' interlanguage fossilized. Although he acquired a high degree of communicative competence, he acquired only a limited degree of grammatical competence.

There have been a number of other studies of the acculturation hypothesis. Some have shown that acculturation variables correlate with language proficiency, others have shown the opposite. An example of the former is Maple (1982), who found that for 190 Spanish-speaking university students social distance, as measured by a questionnaire and an interview, correlated with English proficiency. On the other hand, Kelly (1982) found that for six Spanish speakers who had lived in the United States for at least nine years, acculturation, as measured by a questionnaire, did not correlate with English proficiency. In fact, the subject who showed the greatest acculturation had the least proficient English.

Reviewing these and other studies, Schumann (1984:12) concluded that the acculturation hypothesis was testable in 'theory but not in fact'. He quotes Kelly: 'It is the dynamic, varying, and complexly individual nature of affect which makes the idealized version of the acculturation model difficult to either prove or disprove.' The untestability of the idealized version of the acculturation hypothesis does not imply that there is no relationship between sociocultural factors and second language acquisition. It may be that the nature of this relationship differs greatly with the situation and with the individual. One problem with the research designs of the acculturation hypothesis studies is that no random sampling is used. Perhaps researchers have thought that random sampling was unnecessary because it is seldom used in psychologically oriented studies of language acquisition. But random sampling is not necessary in these studies because cognitive processing is similar in all human beings. Thus, although the ZISA group did not use random sampling, they discovered an invariant order in the acquisition of German word order rules. But sociocultural studies do require random sampling, and also a large number of subjects, because social and psychological factors affect human beings so differently.

In conclusion, researchers such as Schumann, Gatbonton-Segalowitz, Maple, and many others have suggested that interlanguage varieties, like native language varieties, are related to social and psychological factors. Perhaps more carefully designed studies will help us better understand the nature of this relationship.

Chapter 4

AN EXPERIMENTAL STUDY OF BICKERTON'S BIOPROGRAM THEORY APPLIED TO SECOND LANGUAGE ACQUISITION

1. **Bickerton's theory of universals.** Chapter 1 discussed the stative-nonstative distinction (SND), an example of a language universal proposed by Derek Bickerton (1981), whose work in creole studies has implications for all areas of language acquisition. Bickerton's theory is consistent with the experientialist school of psychology (Lakoff and Johnson 1980), which claims that children build language on more basic cognitive structures. According to this theory, before they learn to speak, children create a basic mental representation of their world. In creating this mental model, they depend upon innate ways of perceiving and categorizing experience. At an early age babies are able to perceive different objects in their environment because the human eye is 'wired' to detect the differences in the intensity of light which occur at the edges of an object against a background of a different color. The one-year-old inhabits a world of objects before she has names for them because she is genetically equipped to perceive them. Thus, the child's mental model of the world is built up out of sensory experience, organized in ways that are genetically specified, and language is built on this preexisting mental model. For example, before the child can learn the word Daddy, she must have a clear idea of who Daddy is. This is not to say that the child will use the word in the adult way at first. She may over generalize, calling all men 'daddy', but her reaction to being picked up by the wrong 'daddy' demonstrates loudly and clearly that she has different concepts, though not yet different words, for Daddy and man.

As noted in Chapter 1, Bickerton proposes that genetically transmitted information specifies not only how the senses work, but also, to some extent, how the mind works. An example involves our ability to predicate, to make observations about objects. According to Bickerton, we automatically divide predicates into two types: actions and states of being. Actions include falling, running, meowing; states include being hot or cold, hungry or satisfied. This innate cognitive ability accounts for the ease with which children learn the SND if this distinction happens to be marked in the adult language.

34

Bickerton's universals differ from those proposed by other
scholars. For one thing, not all languages have them. This is because
Bickerton's universals are cognitive rather than purely linguistic. His
claim is that all mature humans are able to make, for example, the
SND; but all languages need not mark this distinction--they will only
have a tendency to do so. A second difference is that knowledge of a
universal is not necessarily present when a child is born. Rather, it
emerges as the child develops. The important point for language
acquisition research is that after a certain point of development,
children will be looking for particular language features. If the target
language has these features, they will be easily acquired.

Bickerton's strongest evidence for the existence of language universals is that they are present in all creole languages, even though they
are usually absent from the parent pidgins. Thus, the children who
expand the pidgin to create the creole do so in a way that conforms to
the natural categories of thought. Additional evidence comes from
child language acquisition. As we have seen, the English progressive
-ing, which makes the SND, is acquired early.

If Bickerton's universals are involved in first language acquisition
and creolization, it is reasonable to suppose that they are involved, at
least to some extent, in second language acquisition and in pidginization as well. We have reviewed several second language acquisition
studies (Dulay and Burt, Cazden et al., the ZISA group) which suggest
that universals of some kind are involved in second language acquisition. However, as mentioned in Chapter 3, Bickerton does not believe
that universals are involved in second language acquisition or in pidginization. His thinking is summed up in the slogan, 'Pidginization is
second language learning with restricted input and creolization is first
language acquisition with restrticted input' (1977:49). For Bickerton,
the initial stages of both pidginization and second language acquisition
involve relexifying the native language, not creating new cognitively
simple structures. Nevertheless, in view of the evidence for universals
in second language acquisition (as well as Kay and Sankoff's 1974
claims about universals in pidginization), the authors[1] of this chapter
decided to examine a sample of interlanguage for evidence of one of
Bickerton's universals.

2. The specific-nonspecific distinction. We chose to examine the
interlanguage of adult Korean speakers for evidence of specific-nonspecific distinction (SNSD)--a second universal proposed by Bickerton.
This distinction applies to NPs, which can be divided into four types
along two dimensions: (1) specific versus nonspecific and (2) known to
the hearer versus unknown, as shown in Figure 4.1. An NP is +specific
and +known if it is a unique reference or is conventionally assumed to
be a unique reference, if the referent is physically present, or if the
referent was previously mentioned in the discourse. All NPs of this
first type are marked with the. An NP is -specific and +known if it
names a generic. Generics can be marked with the, a, or ∅. An NP is
-specific and -known if it is in the scope of negation, irrealis, or question, or is of indefinite number. This third type of NP is marked with a
or ∅. An NP is +specific and -known when it is first mentioned in a
discourse. It is marked with a or ∅. This study is concerned only with

whether an NP is +specific or -specific and does not deal with whether an NP is +known or -known.

Figure 4.1   Types of noun phrases and their uses.

Type	Use	Example
1. +Specific + Known to hearer	1. Unique reference 2. Referent physically present 3. Referent previously mentioned	We saw **the** Pope. Pick up **the** paper. A dog bit me. I didn't see the darn thing coming.
2. -Specific +Known to hearer	Generics	**The** camel is a noble beast. **A** dog is nice to have. ∅ Children like to play.
3. -Specific -Known to hearer	1. Negation 2. Modal, irrealis 3. Questions 4. Indefinite number	I don't have to have **a** party. I would like to have **a** party. Do you want **a** soda? He's always looking for ∅ cans.
4. +Specific -Known to hearer	First mention in discourse	**A** dog bit me. I didn't see the darn thing coming. Today I ate ∅ cookies and a candy bar.

We chose speakers of Korean as our subjects because Korean does not have articles; therefore, we reasoned, these speakers might fall back on innate knowledge when acquiring a language like English that does have articles. If they do, their initial hypothesis about English articles should be the same as the hypothesis of creole-speaking children, namely:

(1)   Use articles to mark +specific NPs; use ∅ to mark -specific NPs.

There is indirect evidence that children use hypothesis (1) when acquiring English as a first language. Maratsos (1976) studied the accuracy of article use by three- and four-year-olds. He found that children understand the SNSD and can make it accurately at the age of three. This is a remarkable achievement since the SNSD is not clearly marked in English. As Figure 4.1 shows, the, a, and ∅ mark both +specific and -specific NPs, as illustrated in the following pairs of sentences.

(2)   **The dog** that barked all night lives next door. (+specific)
(3)   **The dog** is man's best friend. (-specific)

(4)   I saw **a possum** in our yard last night. (+specific)
(5)   Mary can't stand to have **a possum** in the yard. (-specific)

(6)   **Hit lists** were discussed while Speakes was asleep. (+specific)
(7)   It is absolutely untrue that hit lists were discussed while
       Speakes was asleep. (-specific).

The only time that English articles unambiguously mark the SNSD is
when there are two references to an NP. When the first reference uses
a and the second the, the NP is specific, as in (8).

(8)   Bill bought **a cat** and **a possum,** but the children only
       like **the possum.**

Maratsos asked his subjects to complete stories where an NP was not
clearly marked +specific or -specific by articles, but where the semantic content made this information clear. He then tested to find out
if the children had understood whether the NP was +specific or not by
asking them to complete a sentence where they would have to mark
this information by using articles correctly. For example, the children
were read stories like the following (Maratsos 1976:448).

    Once there was a man who went to the jungle to look
    for a lion or a zebra. He looked for a lion or a
    zebra everywhere. He looked and looked. Suddenly,
    who came running out at the man?

Since no specific lion or zebra has been established, the correct answer
is a lion or a zebra. The children were also told a similar story with a
different ending:

    ...then the man found a lion and a zebra together. Who
    came running out at the man? (p. 449)

Here, the correct answer is the lion or the zebra because a specific
antecedent has been established. Maratsos found that children were
remarkably successful in differentiating specific from nonspecific
NPs. The three-year-olds achieved a success rate of 90 percent and
the four-year-olds a rate of over 90 percent.
    Maratsos' experiment is not a direct test of hypothesis (1). To
perform such a test he would have had to compare the errors made by
very young learners to those made by older learners. If the younger
learners, but not the older ones, tended to omit articles more before
nonspecific NPs, this would directly support the hypothesis. What
Maratsos' study does show is that children can accurately mark the
SNSD much earlier than we would expect them to. Maratsos observes
(1976:454): 'Distinctions between before and after ... and more and less
... cause young children much trouble even as they are learning complex syntax. The specific versus nonspecific difference appears to be
an abstract difference as well, yet does not seem to cause much difficulty.' The ease with which children master the SNSD, an abstract
concept which is ambiguously marked in the adult language, suggests

that they are predisposed to look for this feature.

3. The experiment. The subjects in this study were 14 adult Korean speakers who were residents of Northern Virginia in the spring of 1981, when the original project was begun. At that time, they had been living in the United States for various lengths of time, from a few months to several years, and had varying degrees of English proficiency. Figure 4.2 gives a brief description of the subjects.

Figure 4.2 The subjects of the study.

Number in study	Cloze score	Sex	Time in U.S.
1	30	M	5-1/2 yrs.
2	57	F	2-1/2 yrs.
3	61	F	2-1/2 yrs.
4	59	M	12 yrs.
5	42	M	1 yr.
6	55	F	2 yrs.
7	69	M	9 mos.
8	58	F	9 yrs.
9	18	F	7 yrs.
10	15	F	1 yr.
11	33	F	9 yrs.
12	31	F	9 yrs.
13	52	F	5 mos.
14	6	F	5 yrs.

In the spring of 1981, graduate linguistics students at George Mason University interviewed the subjects. They taped the interviews and later transcribed them. Each interviewer asked the subject about her length of residence in the United States, whether or not she was currently studying English, her family, her typical day, and the surroundings in which the interview was being held. In addition to participating in the interview, each subject also took a cloze test to determine roughly that individual's overall English proficiency.

The following spring, with the help of a second group of linguistics graduate students, we scored the transcripts for article usage. We found that our subjects' most common strategy by far was to omit articles. The following examples give some of the flavor of our subjects' interlanguage.

-Q: Can you tell me about your first day in the U.S.?
-A: Well, it's hard to remember about it. Change of time a little bit different.
-In my country man is first Man is always right.
-I can never have friendship with Americans.
-I took grammar course and a writing course.

The first step in our data tabulation was to mark all NPs either +specific or -specific. Repeated NPs and NPs that were in set phrases (such as <u>in the morning</u>) were not counted. Nor did we count proper names or NPs that were marked with other qualifiers (We say **one** dog). Next, the article (if any) used with each NP was noted. In addition, we looked for signs of interference from Korean in the subjects' use of articles. Huebner (1983) discovered that his Hmong-speaking subject did not at first use articles to mark NPs that were sentence subjects. Huebner attributed this strategy to the influence of Hmong, a topic-prominent language which does not attach any marker to a sentence topic. He claimed that his subject first interpreted the as a marker of the sentence topic and thus did not use it before NPs that were sub-jects. Despite the fact that Korean is a topic-prominent language, we found no evidence that this influenced our subjects' interlanguage. The final step in our data tabulation was to count the number of articles used before +specific and before -specific NPs.

Next, we ranked all of our subjects in descending order by the frequency of their article use. It was found that when the subjects did use articles, they used them correctly. There were virtually no instan-ces of their using an incorrect article, a for the or vice versa, or either article or Ø. Thus, frequency of article use was equivalent to accuracy of article use. We then divided the subjects into a high proficiency group and a low proficiency group. The dividing line fell between subjects 8 and 9, as shown in Figure 4.3.

Figure 4.3   How the subjects used articles.

Subject	Overall score	Use/ Contexts +spec	Percent articles supplied	Use/ Contexts -spec	Percent articles supplied	Difference between per-cent +spec and -spec
High proficiency group:						
1	82	24/28	86	4/6	67	19
2	80	20/28	71	35/41	85	-16
3	71	20/27	74	7/11	64	10
4	66	29/41	70	13/22	59	11
5	64	33/53	62	10/14	71	-11
6	63	16/25	64	10/16	63	1
7	57	6/8	75	2/6	33	42
8	45	10/24	42	7/14	50	-12
Low proficiency group:						
9	31	18/54	33	2/11	18	15
10	21	5/16	31	0/8	0	31
11	17	4/16	25	0/8	0	25
12	16	4/24	17	0/1	0	17
13	6	0/32	0	3/17	18	-18
14	5	3/48	6	0/16	0	6

The groups were divided at this point rather than at any other because this was the lowest point at which the high proficiency subjects and low proficiency subjects had significantly different scores.

After the high proficiency and low proficiency groups were formed and all of the data listed, four statistical tests were run to determine the differences in article usage within each group and between the two groups, as outlined in Figure 4.4.

Figure 4.4   Research design.

Test	Independent variable	Dependent variable	Dependent variable
1	Correlation of difference in rank	Rank by accuracy of article use	Rank by cloze score
2	High proficiency in English	Frequency of article use before +spec NPs	Frequency of article use before -spec NPs
3	Low proficiency in English	Frequency of article use before +spec NPs	Frequency of article use before -spec. NPs
4	Comparison of difference	Difference between articles before +spec NPs and -spec NPs in high proficiency group	Difference between articles before +spec NPs and -spec. NPs in low proficiency group

Test 1 (a Spearman's Rho test) was run to determine the correlation between the subjects' rank in article accuracy and overall English proficiency as measured by the cloze test (see Figure 4.5).

Figure 4.5   Subjects ranked by article accuracy and cloze score.

Article accuracy	Cloze score
1	11
2	5
3	2
4	3
5	8
6	6
7	1
8	4
9	12
10	13
11	9
12	10
13	7
14	14

The results (rho = .79, df = 12) showed a significant correlation (at the .05 level) between the subjects' accuracy of article use and their cloze score ranks. This correlation is expected. It means that as a subject's overall English proficiency improves, her accuracy with articles also improves. That there is not a perfect correlation demonstrates that a second language learner can have high overall proficiency in English without having the same level of proficiency for each individual morpheme.

In test 2 (a t-test), the difference between the frequency of article

use before +specific and -specific NPs for the low proficiency group
proved to be slightly less than significant (at the .05 level; t = 1.8, df =
5). This result was somewhat disappointing since hypothesis (1) predicts that low proficiency subjects will use articles more often before
+specific than before -specific NPs. Nevertheless, although statistical
significance was not reached, the low proficiency group did use articles
twice as often before +specific NPs than before -specific NPs (18%
versus 9%). The lack of significance is probably due to the small
number of articles used by this group.

Figure 4.6   All subjects' use of articles before specific NPs
compared to their use of articles before nonspecific
NPs.

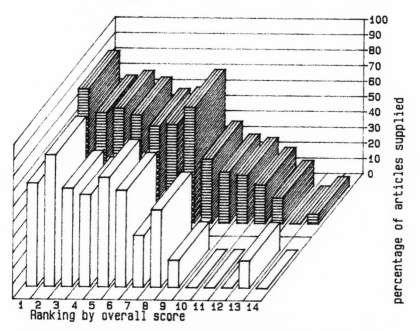

Key   Shaded bars = articles supplied before specific NPs
       Clear bars = articles supplied before nonspecific NPs
       Subjects 1-8 = high proficiency group
       Subjects 9-14 = low proficiency group

In test 3 (also a t-test) the difference between the frequency of
article use in +specific and -specific environments for the high proficiency group proved to be not significant (at the .05 level; t = 1.8, df =
7), as expected. We can be confident of these results since the high
proficiency group used many more articles than did the low proficiency
group.

Test 4 (an analysis of variance) measured the difference in the
difference between article use before +specific and -specific NPs in
the high proficiency group and the low proficiency group. In other

words, it answered the question: compared to the high proficiency group, did the low proficiency group use articles more often before +specific NPs than before -specific NPs? This was the crucial test of hypothesis (1). Let us examine more closely what it measured. We know that the high proficiency group used articles with about equal frequency before +specific and -specific NPs. We know that the low proficiency group used articles with greater frequency before +specific NPs than before -specific NPs (although due to the small number of tokens this difference was not quite significant). Test 4, then, measured the difference between these two frequencies. The difference proved to be significant (at the .05 level; f = 19.9, df = 1 and 12). These results support hypothesis (1).

These findings suggest that Bickerton's universals may, to some extent, influence second language acquisition. Lacking a hypothesis about how to use articles from their native language, the Korean-speaking subjects assumed that articles marked the SNSD. Thus like creole speakers, they tended to use articles only to mark +specific NPs. As they became more proficient in English, they revised their hypothesis about how articles work and adopted hypotheses more like the actual English rules.

Note

1. This chapter is the result of a research project begun by Adamson, who collected the data with the help of Mary Ciske and other graduate students. The data analysis was done primarily by Ciske, who is coauthor of this chapter.

Chapter 5

LINGUISTIC RULES AND PSYCHOLOGICAL REALITY

1. **Linguistics and psychology.** Linguistics has always been influenced by its sister discipline psychology, but this relationship has been especially close since the 1960s, when Chomsky (1965) declared that the goal of linguistics was to describe how humans acquire and use language. To achieve this goal, Chomsky set down the outlines for a science of the mind. Prior to Chomsky, linguists had been influenced by behaviorist psychologists, who forebade speculations about mental structures and processes. Most behaviorists did not deny that humans had minds; but they claimed that since the mind could not be observed, it was fruitless to speculate about how it might work. Behaviorists proposed to study only observable events, namely, the behavior of organisms and its relationship to the environment in which that behavior occurred. The relationship between environment and behavior was modeled in the formula Stimulus → Response, which says that similar behaviors (responses) follow similar stimuli (environments). Thus, the behaviorists believed that if stimuli could be thoroughly understood, responses could be predicted. The behaviorists were successful in making accurate predictions about the behavior of small animals, such as rats, in very controlled laboratory conditions, such as mazes. But they were not successful in making accurate predictions about how human beings behave. This failure led to the decline of radical behaviorism.

The behaviorists' decline was hastened, in part, by Chomsky's (1959) famous attack on B.F. Skinner's major work Verbal Behavior. Chomsky objected to Skinner's claim that the stimulus-response mechanism by which rats learn mazes was essentially the same mechanism by which humans learn languages, and that animal behavior could be extrapolated into a model of human behavior. He also claimed that it was possible to study the workings of the mind scientifically. The model of human mental processes which is sometimes implicit in Chomsky's writing (e.g. 1959:29) is the computer. The computational model of mental processes has been adopted by many linguists and psychologists, who sometimes use computer terminology to describe human mental processes. Hamburger and Crain (1984), for example, compare the mental processes involved in understanding a command to the computa-

43

tional processes involved in compiling a program. Similarly, Anderson (1980) compares mentally planning a sentence to executing a series of programmed 'production rules', as discussed in Section 3 of this chapter. In fact, the computer model of language processing has been so attractive that a new discipline largely based on this model has emerged: 'cognitive science' draws upon psychology, linguistics, and artificial intelligence to investigate mental structures and processes in mind and machine.

The way in which a computer works can be explained on several different levels. On one level, what happens within the computer is described physically: which circuits are on and off during every moment of the computer's operation. The brain's workings could be described physically as well. In theory, one could specify which neurons are activated and in which order when a speaker utters or comprehends a sentence. Unfortunately, brain scientists are very far from being able to describe the brain's workings on this basic physical level. However, cognitive scientists point out that there are more abstract levels on which to describe what a computer (or brain) does. Many people who work with computers understand little of the machine's hardware, but they do understand the software, or the logic of what the machine does. These people are, of course, programmers. They can provide an explicit step-by-step description of the computer's operation when, say, it makes out a payroll. Programmers treat the computer as an information processing device: they tell the machine what information to store and how to manipulate that information.

The brain, too, might be considered an information processing device which may work according to some kind of program, which, in this analogy, is the mind. A possible goal for cognitive psychology and for linguistics is to discover how this program works. Grammarians might try to write an explicit description of how the mind processes grammatical information. But Chomsky did not adopt this goal. Under his influence, linguistics became aligned with cognitive psychology as a mentalistic science, but the alignment was far from complete. In fact, Chomsky's goals differed dramatically from those of cognitive psychology, as we will see.

Chomsky attempted to represent a speaker's knowledge of a language by linguistic rules which described the grammatical patterns of the language. For example, rule (1) states that a determiner may precede a noun.

(1)   NP ⟶ (det) + N

Everyone agrees that English conforms to rule (1), but the question remains whether the rule says anything interesting about how the mind stores or processes linguistic information. If rule (1) can be part of a process description or model of what happens mentally when we produce or understand a sentence, it is said to have 'psychological reality'. However, Chomsky claimed that the question of whether a linguistic description had psychological reality could be settled without recourse to psychological experiments or 'external evidence'. Instead, psychological reality could be tested by the 'internal evidence' of the system the linguist constructed. The simplest and most consistent set of rules would be the psychologically real set, presumably because such rules would be the most efficient for encoding and decoding language and would be easiest to learn.[1]

Chomsky's goal, then, was to construct a simple and consistent system of rules which would specify the grammatical sentences of the language. To accomplish this goal, he employed certain ideas used in mathematics. First, he noted that a language contains an infinite number of grammatical sentences. In this respect, a language is like the set of even integers, which is also infinite. Previous linguists, like Saussure, had despaired at this great diversity: how could something infinite ever be described? Chomsky knew that such a task is common in mathematics. For example, it is possible to describe the set of even integers by means of equation (2).

(2) $X = 2Y$
where X is an even integer
and Y is any integer

Equation (2) is said to 'generate' the set of even integers. This does not mean that the equation produces them in a physical sense, the way a turbine produces electricity. Rather 'generate' is used in the special mathematical sense of 'defining' or 'specifying' the set of even integers. It is possible to test whether any number is a member of the set of even integers by plugging it into the X value and seeing if the equation will balance.

Chomskian linguists attempt to write a set of equation-like rules which will, in this technical sense, generate all and only the sentences of a language. A brief fragment of these rules might look like the rules in Figure 5.1.

Figure 5.1   Generative rules for the sentences: <u>The man bit the dog</u> and <u>The dog bit the man</u>.

Phrase structure rules	Lexical rules
1. S ---> NP + VP	4. det ---> the
2. NP ---> det + N	5. N ---> man, dog
3. VP ---> V + NP	6. V ---> bit

The rules in Figure 5.1 generate sentences (3) and (4).

(3)   The man bit the dog.
(4)   The dog bit the man.

These rules do not generate sentence (5).

(5)   *The man the dog bit.

Although the rules in Figure 5.1 are numbered, they are not supposed to apply in real time. This is because they do not physically produce sentences; instead, like equation (2), they exist all at the same time to specify which sentences are possible. Just as equation (2) defines a set

of numbers, the rules in Figure 5.1 define a (very small) set of sentences. Chomsky showed that with the addition of other rules it is possible to generate an infinite number of sentences.

Chomsky's generative grammar has been misunderstood as a model
of how the human mind or a computer program might produce sentences, instead of as a quasi-mathematical specification of what sentences
are possible in a language. Chomsky calls his grammar a 'competence
grammar' to distinguish it from a mental grammar or a computer
program, which would be a 'performance grammar'. Chomsky uses
'competence', like 'generate', in a special technical sense. A competence grammar is a 'formal system', like Euclidean geometry. Specifi-
cally, it is a kind of Post System, named after the American mathema-
tician Emile Post (see Lakoff forthcoming for discussion). A human
being or a machine cannot have competence in this special sense. The
word refers only to the nature and power of a set of rules. Thus, the
goal of Chomskian linguistics--to construct a competence grammar--
differed drastically from the goal of cognitive psychology--to construct
a performance grammar, a psychologically real model of language
processing.

The different goals required different research methods. The
Chomskian linguist could theoretically construct a competence grammar without leaving her arm chair. She had only to consult her own
intuitions about which sentences were or were not grammatical and
then write a set of rules to generate these sentences. The psychologist, on the other hand, had to produce experimental or observational
evidence of which proposed rules or other structures best seemed to
model human mental processes. Are irregular past tense verbs learned
individually or are they produced from very abstract underlying forms,
as generative phonology suggests? Is there a mental process that
corresponds to moving elements around in a sentence, the way transformations do, or is it better to think of the mind storing sentence
patterns as phrase structure rules?

Unfortunately, there has been massive confusion about the competence-performance distinction because many people, including
Chomsky himself on occasion,[2] use 'competence' in its everyday sense,
not in its technical sense. For example, aphasics who have lost the
ability to speak but who still understand and write perfectly well, are
said to have competence but to lack performance. Also, language
learners who can sometimes but not always produce a complex form
like the passive are said to have the competence to produce the form,
but to fail sometimes because of performance factors. This distinction
between capability and actual production is a useful one, especially for
language acquisition scholars, but it must not be confused with
Chomsky's competence-performance distinction.

A competence grammar is not without value to a psychologist, as
we will see, but it is not as useful as was once hoped. In the 1960s a
number of psychological experiments--for example, Savin and
Perchonock (1965)--suggested that competence rules could be adapted
in a straightforward way into performance rules, which would model
what a mind or a program does when it produces a sentence. However,
it soon became apparent that Chomsky's 'standard theory', as outlined
in Aspects of the Theory of Syntax (1965) did not reflect mental pro-

cesses in any obvious way. For one thing, Chomsky's model implies that when speakers want to say something, they begin with a syntactic form, such as rule (1), rather than with the idea of what they want to say. Intuitively, this procedure seems backwards. For another thing, the grammar suggests that sentences to which many transformations have applied are more complex and therefore take longer to process mentally than sentences to which few transformations have applied. This 'derivational complexity theory' also predicts that children learn to say sentences closer to underlying structure before they learn to say sentences involving more transformations. If this were true, children should learn full passives like My cat got run over by something before they learn truncated passives like My cat got run over. This proved not to be the case.

When it became clear that a competence grammar could not be converted in a straightforward way into a psychologically real performance grammar, many psychologists gave up on linguistics as an empirical discipline. However, perhaps this conclusion was premature. We will now consider how competence rules can suggest corresponding performance rules, which are testable claims about how the mind processes language.

2. Declarative knowledge and procedural knowledge. Psychologists divide knowledge into two types: declarative and procedural (Anderson 1980). Declarative knowledge includes facts about the world, such as the fact that Columbus discovered America or that birds eat worms. Procedural knowledge involves knowing how to do something like play tennis or speak a language. Declarative knowledge is knowing that, procedural knowledge is knowing how. A discussion of performance rules involves procedural knowledge, but we first briefly consider declarative knowledge because it will be useful later on.

One model of how declarative knowledge is represented in the mind is the schema. Rosch (1973) claimed that some natural categories such as BIRD and TREE are stored in long-term memory as schemas--complex units of knowledge containing related information. One kind of schema is the 'prototype'. Prototype theory claims that we know what a bird is because our minds abstract properties or features from all the birds we have encountered to construct a 'most typical' or prototype bird. If we encounter a new feathered creature, we compare it to our prototype for BIRD in order to decide whether it is a bird or not. Rosch found that her subjects' prototype schemas for BIRD were very similar. She showed subjects pictures of various birds and asked them which were the most typical. Subjects agreed that robins were very typical but chickens were not. This finding suggests that robins are closer than chickens to the mental prototype BIRD.

A second type of schema is called a 'script'. Scripts are mental representations of a connected experience, such as going to a restaurant. In order to act appropriately in a restaurant, one must draw on knowledge of what a typical restaurant experience is like. The restaurant script includes entering the restaurant, getting a table, summoning the waiter, examining the menu, and so on. Not all cultures share the same restaurant script. For example, part of a Spaniard's restaurant script involves summoning the waiter by raising one's hand and saying in a loud whisper, 'Pssst'.

Bower, Black, and Turner (1979) tested the psychological reality of Americans' restaurant scripts by having subjects study stories about restaurants which included some but not all of the typical restaurant events. When subjects were subsequently asked to tell whether certain statements about these typical events actually came from the story, they were unable to do so. Instead, they tended to report that information from their internal restaurant scripts was part of the story they had read.

A different kind of mental construct is required to model procedural knowledge. Psychologists and artificial intelligence researchers write programs containing 'production systems' which can be run on a computer but which are also supposed to model how the mind processes language. Here productions are discussed as they might work on a computer, but the discussion is intended to have relevance to human mental processes as well. Anderson (1980:239) gives the production for shifting from first to second gear in a three-speed car, shown in (6).

(6)   IF   a car is in first gear
            and the car is going faster than 10 mph
            and there is a clutch
            and there is a stick
     THEN depress the clutch
            and move the stick to the upper right position
            and release the clutch.

A production, then, consists of one or more conditions and one or more actions.

Anderson notes the similarity of productions and morphological rules. As an example of this similarity, a production for pluralizing regular English nouns that end in a voiceless consonant (other than a sibilant) is shown in (7).

(7)   IF   the noun is not marked as irregular
            and the noun ends in a voiceless consonant
            and the voiceless consonant is not
            a sibilant
     THEN attach /s/ to the end of the noun

This production is similar to the linguistic rule shown in (8), which says: the plural morpheme is realized as /s/ following a voiceless sibilant.

(8)   PLURAL -->/s/ $\bigg/ \begin{bmatrix} \text{-voice} \\ \text{-sibilant} \end{bmatrix}$ + _____

Production (7) and performance rule (8) contain basically the same information, but in (7) the information is encoded procedurally and in (8) it is encoded declaratively. Furthermore, both rule and production make the same basic psychological claim: regular plural forms are not learned individually but are produced from base forms of nouns. Note that neither production nor rule is necessarily psychologically real. It is logically possible that humans do learn the plural forms of nouns on a word-by-word basis and store these forms in memory separately. However, Berko (1958), in her famous <u>wugs</u> experiment, demonstrated that this is not the case. Instead, regular plurals are produced by rules which apply to the base forms of nouns. Thus, both (7) and (8) are helpful in understanding how humans produce language and therefore have some degree of psychological reality.

Rules like (8), then, are useful to psychologists. They can be considered descriptions, at an abstract level, of what the mind does when it plans a word or sentence. However, if a rule makes such a psychological claim it must be considered a performance rule, not a competence rule, and ideally should be supported by acquisitional or experimental evidence. But although the performance rules and competence rules are very different conceptually, in practice they are not so far apart. For one thing, rule (8) was first constructed as a competence rule, which turned out to be a useful description of language production. Also, any scientific theory should, in addition to being true, be simple and consistent. So these considerations should apply to performance rules as well as to competence rules as long as theoretical conventions are consistent with empirical evidence.

3. Competence rules, performance rules and productions. Now consider a syntactic example of the relationship between competence rules, performance rules, and productions. As has been seen, the competence rules in Figure 5.1 generate (9).

(9)   The man bit the dog.

How do these rules correspond to a production system and to a set of performance rules? Sentence production begins with the meaning a speaker wishes to express. Meanings (like declarative knowledge) can be stated as a series of logical propositions. For example, the basic meaning of (9) can be represented as in (10), where the semantic roles of the NPs are labeled. Psychologists have used the notation shown in (10a), whereas linguists are perhaps more familiar with the notation in (10b). Figure 5.2 shows how productions and performance rules can be equivalent by showing how each would change (10) into sentence (9). The productions are shown on the left side of Figure 5.2 and the equivalent performance rules on the right side.

(10a)

(10b) $(bit)_{Verb} \left((man)_{Agent} \quad (dog)_{Object} \right)$

The first step in a production system for transforming proposition (10) into sentence (9) is to recognize that the semantic information con-

Figure 5.2 A comparison of a production and the equivalent performance rules. The production assumes that the program which uses it already has the semantic representation shown in proposition (10) of Chapter 5.

Productions	Performance Rules	
Name and (form) of production	Rule	Result
Clause 1 (IF it is to be asserted that an agent performed an action on an object THEN plan to say a string of the form) Agent+Verb+Object result: man bit dog Agent	P1. S→ Agent+Verb+Object	$((man)_{Agent}+(bit)_{Verb}+(dog)_{Object})S$
	P2. Agent→ NP	$(((man)_{NP}+(bit)_{Verb}+(dog)_{Object})S)_{Agent}$
Noun phrase (IF it is supposed that a case role is a noun THEN plan to say the+ noun) result: The man bit dog	P3. NP→ the+N	$((((the (man)_N)+(bit)_{Verb}+(dog)_{Object})S)_{NP})_{Agent}$
Noun phrase (repeat above process) result: The man bit the dog	P4. Object→ NP	

tained in (10) can be expressed as a single clause. In order to do this, the computer must know that a clause can consist of an Agent, Verb, and Object. This information is contained in the computer's memory and is not represented in the first production, called 'clause'. Having recognized that (10) can be expressed as a clause, the computer then fires the clause production which specifies the correct order of Agent, Verb, and Object. So, the machine moves the word filling the Agent role--<u>man</u>--to the first position, followed by the Verb <u>bit</u> and then the Object <u>dog</u>. The clause production logically does two things: it produces the string <u>man</u> + <u>bit</u> + <u>dog</u> and identifies this string as a clause. This same information can be expressed in more traditional linguistic terms by performance rule (P1).

Continuing on the production side of Figure 5.2, the computer now looks to see whether it should fire the 'noun phrase' production. It will do this whenever it finds a case role expressed as a noun. In order to recognize a noun, the computer must have in its memory a lexicon which lists all the words in the language with their part of speech. This lexical information is not contained in the productions nor in the performance rules in Figure 5.2. Lexical information, then, is not procedural knowledge: it is declarative knowledge which, in human beings, is stored in long-term memory. Thus, procedural knowledge is not independent of declarative knowledge. A major question in psycholinguistics is how these two kinds of knowledge interact. The production system in Figure 5.2 is very specific about what knowledge is declarative (and so stored in long term-memory) and what knowledge is procedural (and so part of the production). For example, as noted, the information that a clause can consist of an Agent, Verb, and Object is in long-term memory. The information that the correct order of these elements is Agent + Verb + Object is in the Noun Phrase production. The performance rules in Figure 5.2 are less specific about this division of knowledge. Both pieces of information mentioned here (the possible elements in a clause and the correct ordering of those elements) are contained in rule (P1). The performance rules allow various possibilities for realizing their information in a production model.

Continuing the Noun Phrase production in Figure 5.2, the computer looks at the word which fills the Agent case role; consulting its lexicon, it sees that <u>man</u> is a noun, so it puts <u>the</u> in front of <u>man</u>. Logically, the Noun Phrase production does three things: it labels the Agent, <u>man</u>, as a noun; it puts <u>the</u> in front of the noun; and it labels this two-word string a noun phrase. This information is expressed by performance rules (P2) and (P3). In the last step, the computer continues to look for case roles that are expressed as nouns. It finds that <u>bit</u> does not fill a case role (Verb is not a case role), so it goes on to <u>dog</u>. Since <u>dog</u> does fill a case role (Object), and furthermore is a noun, the 'noun phrase' production fires again, creating the string <u>the dog</u>, and in effect labeling it a noun phrase. This information is shown in rule (P4) which produces an NP, which in turn is followed by a reapplication of rule (P3), completing the string.

Notice that productions are more explicit than performance rules. They constitute an algorithm for translating propositions into grammatical strings of words. Performance rules are more abstract; there are presumably a number of production systems which could embody the information contained in performance rules. Yet, since we know almost nothing about the mind's production systems (or, indeed, if the mind uses anything like production systems), it may be that performance rules are at a very useful level of abstraction for discussions of cognitive processes at this stage in the development of psycholinguistics. Competence rules, on the other hand, are not suited for use in a psycholinguistic theory since they are not intended to model mental operations, and are not subject to empirical verification. Nevertheless, as we have seen, these rules can contain information that is helpful to psycholinguists.

4. Evidence for psychological reality. Consider now two examples of experimental evidence which tend to support the claims made by the language production model suggested by Figure 5.2. One claim is that the clause is the basic unit of planning in sentence production. Evidence supporting this claim comes from Fromkin's (1973) analysis of slips of the tongue. Fromkin observed such errors as The bancer took my dike (instead of The dancer took my bike). The speaker who said the first sentence was obviously anticipating the /b/ of bike when she pronounced bancer. This transposition suggests that at some level of mental organization bike was already being processed while the speaker was attempting to say dancer. Fromkin's evidence is also interesting for what it does not contain. She found that slips of the tongue are not likely to occur across constituent boundaries. We find few sentences like: *The course that the how frightened ran away (instead of The horse that the cow frightened ran away). This is because cow is in the dependent clause and horse is in the independent clause. This evidence suggests that a basic unit in sentence planning is the clause.

Additional, though less direct, support for the model of language production in Figure 5.2 comes from experiments involving verbal memory. Figure 5.2 implies that the way the mind stores meaning can be modeled by propositions, such as proposition (10). Thus, what we hear or read is remembered in terms of propositions, not sentences or words. This theory implies that comprehending is the reverse of the process shown in Figure 5.2. When we comprehend, we convert strings of words into propositions. If this is so, it should take longer to comprehend a string of words which contains many propositions than a string of words which contains few propositions, even though the number of words is about the same. To find out if this is so, Kintch and Keenan (1973, Kintch 1977) had subjects read paragraphs silently and then recall as much of the paragraph as they could. They predicted that the time required to read and understand a paragraph would depend more on the number of propositions than on the number of words. Thus, it should take longer to process (12), which contains eight propositions, than to process (11), which contains only four, though both contain about the same number of words.

(11)   Romulus, the legendary founder of Rome, took the women of the Sabines by force.

(12)   Cleopatra's downfall lay in her foolish trust in the fickle political figures of the Roman world.

The results of Kintch and Keenan's experiment showed that processing time was increased more by the number of propositions than by the number of words. Depending on the length of the passage, each additional proposition increased the reading time between 1.5 and 4.5 seconds.

5. Summary. This chapter has described how in the last 20 years linguistics has become a cognitive science, largely due to the influence of Chomsky. However, Chomsky's goals and methods are very different from those of cognitive psychologists. In particular, Chomsky's competence grammar cannot be a cognitive model since it is not subject to empirical validation. However, patterns discovered by Chomskian linguists, such as the rule for plural formation, can be very useful to psycholinguists. These patterns can be expressed as performance rules, abstract descriptions of how the mind processes language. Performance rules can be tested for psychological reality, as in the work of Berko, Fromkin, and Kintch and Keenan, and translated into explicit real time models in the form of productions. Chapters 6 and 7 describe how variable performance rules might be useful in a model of cognitive processes.

Notes

1. Stabler (1984) discusses two assumptions which underlie the claim that the mental grammar is the simplest grammar. The first is that the simplest mental representation is the most efficient for understanding and producing sentences. But Chomskian simplicity does not seem to coincide with computer efficiency. Stabler points out that Marcus' sentence parser uses shortcuts and heuristics that are contrary to a logically simple model. The second assumption is that a simple model is more easily learned by children. Stabler points out that this is not necessarily so because of Chomsky's own point that children are born with some knowledge of what languages are like. Thus, 'simple' is a relative term; it depends on what you already know, and simplicity may be very different for children, grammarians, and computers.

2. Unfortunately, Chomsky often talks about people having competence. He assumes (1965:9) that 'No doubt, a reasonable model of language use will incorporate, as a basic component, the generative grammar that expresses a speaker-hearer's knowledge of the language; but this generative grammar does not, in itself prescribe the character or functioning of a perceptual model or a model of speech production.' But the problem (the 'realization problem') is exactly how a generative grammar can be part of a performance grammar. Bresnan (1978:2) makes the obvious suggestion that generative grammars must be revised to be consistent with psycholinguistic research. But if this is done, it is not clear how a competence grammar differs from a performance grammar. For a discussion of the technical meaning versus the ordinary meaning of 'competence', see Fillmore (1979:91), who suggests that 'the distinction between competence and performance may not be as important for a larger understanding of language behavior as some scholars have considered it to be.' For a collection of quotes from Chomsky illustrating his interchangeable use of the two meanings of 'competence', see Dreyfus (1972:236).

Chapter 6

THE PSYCHOLOGICAL REALITY OF VARIABLE RULES

In this chapter and the next, a psychological interpretation of variable rules is considered. The main concern is to provide a psychological explanation of linguistic constraints on a rule. We will see that constraints on a phonological rule can reflect the articulatory difficulty of pronouncing a sound sequence, and that constraints on a syntactic rule can reflect the processing difficulty of producing a sentence. This processing difficulty can result in restrictive simplication.

1. The necessity of variable rules. There is an obvious reason why variable rules are needed in a theory of language acquisition. The performance rules (and productions) that have been discussed are categorical, like competence rules. The rule for plurals discussed in Chapter 5, Section 2 says that nouns ending in a voiceless nonsibilant always take /s/ (unless there is a slip of the tongue). Perhaps this is an accurate description of the speech of some adult native speakers (though this is debatable), but it cannot model the plural production of a child or a nonnative speaker who has not yet mastered this rule. An acquirer must pass from one stage to another and there are often long periods when forms from both stages coexist. Variable rules allow us to model this transition period between an earlier and a later rule, as shown in the discussion of the wave model in Chapter 2.

White (1982) makes a valiant attempt to reconcile Chomsky's Extended Standard Theory with the data of language acquisition, but has to admit the necessity of variable rules.[1]

> If the in-between stage in plural acquisition is seen as a case of optional or variable (Labov, 1969) rule operation, then the change is between two grammars, one of which has no rule of plural marking and the other of which does. This rule itself changes from being optional to obligatory (p.50).

White does not realize Kay's point, discussed in Chapter 2, that variable rules are conceptually different from optional rules and are not allowed in a competence grammar. Thus, the variable rule--considered as a performance, not a competence, rule--is necessary for describing the acquisition of a linguistic structure.

2. The psycholinguistic correlates of constraints. What are the psycholinguistic correlates of the constraints on a variable rule in interlanguage? As a first step one might ask: what are the psycholinguistic correlates of constraints on a variable rule in native speaker speech? One factor is ease of articulation. To return to a familiar example, Wolfram and Fasold (1974) observed that final consonant deletion is more frequent when the following word starts with a consonant instead of a vowel. This is because it is harder to pronounce two consonants together than a consonant followed by a vowel. To get a feel for the truth of this observation try saying, without any deletion, sand castle and then wild elephant. Most people find wild elephant easier to pronounce. As noted in Chapter 1, the theory of natural phonology is based on the premise that certain phonetic patterns are universally easier to pronounce than others.

One would expect difficulty of articulation to cause phonetic variation in interlanguage as well as in native language. In fact, one would expect difficulty of articulation to cause even more phonetic variation in interlanguage, since second language learners must overcome not only universally difficult phonetic patterns, but also some of the phonetic patterns of their native language. Dickerson (1975) studied the acquisition of English phonemes by ten Japanese students studying ESL at an American university. She found that [ɖ] was produced more frequently in some linguistic environments than in others. In the early stages of acquisition, subjects always produced [z] instead of [ɖ]. In later stages, forms similar to [ɖ] emerged, including [dz], [d], and [d] . These fronted forms were more frequent intervocalically than word initially. Although Dickerson did not tabulate the sound before the word-initial /ɖ/, in many cases this sound must have been a consonant, thus producing a consonant cluster. Since CC sequences are harder to produce than VC sequences (especially for speakers of Japanese), we would expect Dickerson's subjects to produce the new sound more frequently in the easier intervocalic environment, as they did. Dickerson's finding agrees with that of Gatbonton-Segalowitz (1976), discussed in Chapter 2, Section 5, who found that the intervocalic environment favored the production of /ɖ/ by French speakers learning English. Thus, one psychological explanation of constraints on variable phonological rules is that they can indicate the relative difficulty of articulation in different environments.

It is less obvious what constraints on morphological and syntactic rules indicate. One possibility is that these constraints reflect the processing difficulty of producing a form. In the discussion of the ZISA group's research in Chapter 3, Section 3, it was noted that restrictive simplification involves omitting an element in a sentence in order to make the sentence easier to process. For example, a low proficiency German acquirer might be able to produce a sentence with a fronted adverb, but at the expense of omitting a copula. This speaker's interlanguage rule could be a variable rule for adverb-initial sentences where copula absence is a favoring constraint.

Another study supporting the hypothesis that variable constraints can reflect processing complexity is that of Adamson and Kovac (1981), who analyzed Schumann's (1978) data on Alberto's use of <u>don't</u> (see Chapter 3, Section 6) and found that Alberto was more likely to negate with <u>don't</u> than with <u>no</u> in sentences that appear less cognitively complex. Recall that Alberto was a 33-year-old immigrant from Costa Rica who was acquiring English without formal instruction while living in Cambridge, Massachusetts. He was one of the six Spanish speakers studied in the Harvard University project (Cazden, Rosansky, Schumann, and Cancino 1975), discussed in Chapter 1, Section 3. Five of the Spanish speakers in Cazden et al. appeared to pass through the following stages for producing sentential negation:

Stage 1	<u>no</u> + verb	I no understand.
Stage 2	<u>don't</u> + verb	He don't like it.
Stage 3	Aux + Neg	They can't do it.
Stage 4	analyzed <u>don't</u>	He doesn't live here.

However, Alberto never progressed beyond stage 2.

Schumann (1978) does the great service of providing an appendix with all of the negative sentences uttered by Alberto during the ten months of the study, a total of 449 negatives. This large amount of data can be analyzed by using the Cedergren-Sankoff VARB Rule 2 computer program (Cedergren and Sankoff 1974), which is discussed below in more detail. For now, it is only necessary to know that the program analyzes variable data in order to test the validity of a linguist's hypothesis about whether a variable rule can describe the data, and (if it can) which of several proposed variable rules fits the data best. The program does not analyze raw data and construct a variable rule. After discussing how the program analyzes the variable rule which describes Alberto's production of English sentential negatives, we will consider a psychological explanation for what the computer analysis finds.

Alberto has two ways of making negative sentences, corresponding to negative stages 1 and 2. Schumann notes that <u>don't</u> is simply a variant of <u>no</u> and does not consist of auxiliary <u>do</u> + Neg. Thus, Alberto appears to have the variable rule:

(1) <u>no</u> ---> (<u>don't</u>)/ NP ___ V (complement)

The VARB Rule 2 program can help discover whether this rule shows environmental stratification (that is, whether it is more likely to apply in certain environments) by isolating the environmental factors which favor the application of the rule (the constraints) and ranking them in order of their importance.

The first step in using the program to analyze Alberto's data is to see if there are any environments in which rule (1) never applies. It appears that there is such an environment. Twenty-three percent of Alberto's negative sentences contain no subject. Thus, Alberto says:

No drink nothing.
No understand.
No have sister.

In these negatives without a subject, don't is supplied only six times--so few that we can claim that Alberto has a separate rule which produces no + VP in these cases. Therefore, subjectless negative sentences are excluded from analysis.

The next step in implementing the program is to make an initial hypothesis about which environmental factors favor the rule. In the analysis of the phonological rule for final stop deletion in Detroit Black English (discussed in Chapter 2, Section 3), only constraints in the environments preceding and following the final stop were found. However, for a syntactic rule one would expect to find constraints in other positions as well since rule application may depend on the overall syntactic complexity of the sentence.

The VARB Rule 2 program requires that the proposed constraints be grouped together into factor groups according to their position in the sentence. Since Alberto's sentences are short, and since there are far fewer data than we would like, only three factor groups will be used: subject position, verb position, and complement position. It is necessary to list exhaustively list all the elements (factors) which can occur in each factor group. These elements will be the proposed constraints, and the program will help determine whether they are real constraints. The factor groups and the factors that can occur in each group are as follows:

Group 1: Subject. Forty-four percent of Alberto's negative sentences contain the subject I. He uses other subjects so infrequently that they must be lumped together into the category 'other subject'.

Group 2: Verb. The most common verbs used by Alberto are be, have, like, and can. Be is not included in the analysis since it should be divided into its various present tense forms and, so divided, there are too few tokens to tabulate. Similarly, the few tokens of will, could, and might are discarded. Other verbs such as understand, speak, play are tabulated under the category MV.

Group 3: Complement. The most frequent complements are nouns, pronouns, no complement, adverbs, and embedded sentences (with that complementizer or infinitive complementizer, frequently reduced). Adverbs, adjectives, and embedded sentences seldom occur, so they must be lumped together in the category 'other'. This analysis is shown in Figure 6.1.

Figure 6.1   Results of the Cedergren-Sankoff program run on all data in the 10-month period.

Subject environment		Verb environment		Complement environment	
I =	.581	can =	.642	Noun =	.592
Other subj. =	.419	MV =	.603	None =	.541
		like =	.570	Other =	.504
		have =	.217	Pronoun =	.365
Input = .518; average chi square = 1.0					

The proposed constraints are not as specific as we would like, and some ad hoc lumping together has occurred. However, perhaps the analysis is fine enough to discover environmental stratification if it exists.

Having set up the factor groups and the factors within each group, we now tabulate how many times Alberto applied rule (1) in all the possible linguistic environments, that is, in all the possible combinations of factors allowed by the analysis. This tabulation requires setting up a chart like Figure 6.2. To construct this chart, we take the first combination of factors, I + can Verb + Ø, and we indicate both the total number of negatives that occurred in this environment and the number of those negatives that contained don't.

Figure 6.2   A partial tabulation of how often Alberto used don't in each possible environment.

Factor group 1	Factor group 2	Factor group 3	Times don't was used	Times don't or no was used
I	can + Verb	Ø	6	10
		Noun	3	3
		Pronoun	3	10
		Other	2	3
	have	Ø	...	...
		Noun	5	10
		Pronoun	0	2
		Other	...	...
.		.		.
.		.		.
.		.		.

After tabulating the data in this way for the entire ten-month period of Schumann's study, a total of 345 negative utterances, the program can be run. If Alberto's interlanguage had changed greatly during the ten months, this procedure would not be justified, since we might be combining several different systems. But Schumann claims that Alberto's interlanguage is relatively stable. Before looking at the initial results, let us briefly consider how the VARB Rule 2 program analyzes the data given to it.

The VARB Rule 2 program assumes that each constraint on a rule is independent of the other constraints. For example, it assumes that the proposed constraint I always contributes the same probability to rule (1) application, regardless of which verb or complement I occurs with. In many other probabilistic situations, different contributing factors operate entirely independently of others. An example is the event that two coins will turn up heads. Whether one coin turns up heads or tails in no way affects how the other coin will land. However, sometimes contributing events do interact. If taking medicine A has a 50 percent probability of curing a patient, and taking medicine B has a 50 percent probability, we cannot assume that taking both medicines will result in an even greater chance of a cure. The two medicines may interact fatally, producing a zero percent chance of a cure. However, many studies have shown that linguistic constraints often do act independently on variable rules (see Cedergren and Sankoff 1974).

The VARB Rule 2 program calculates the contribution (positive or negative) of each proposed constraint toward the application of a variable rule. Proposed constraints which favor rule application are assigned a decimal number between .5 and 1.0, with a higher number indicating a stronger influence. Proposed constraints which disfavor rule application are assigned a decimal number between .5 and 0.0, with a lower number indicating a stronger influence. The computer analysis of Alberto's data produces the results shown in Figure 6.1. The proposed constraint $\underline{I}$ is weighted .581, indicating that it favors rule (1), whereas other subjects disfavor it. The relative weights of the other proposed constraints are indicated by the decimal number following each proposed constraint, as explained above. Two other numbers in Figure 6.1 have yet to be mentioned. The first is the 'Input', which has a value of 5.18. This figure has no theoretical significance; but for complex reasons it must be calculated to allow the program to get on with its work. The second unexplained number is the 'average chi square score', which does have theoretical significance. The average chi square score measures how well the proposed constraints actually fit the data. A high average chi square score indicates that the fit is not good and that the proposed constraints are probably not correct. A low chi square score, on the other hand, indicates that the proposed constraints are probably the correct ones. The average chi square score of 1.04 in Figure 6.2 is too high to allow much confidence in the analysis. We would prefer an average chi square score well below 1.0. Nevertheless, the fit is good enough to indicate that we are on the right track. Clearly, the association between rule (1) and the proposed constraints is far from random.

A possible reason for the relatively high chi square score is that the constraints on rule (1) have changed during the course of the ten months. New constraints may have entered the picture or old constraints may have become reweighted. If such a change in Alberto's internal grammar occurred, it would likely be accompanied by a change in the output of rule (1). It is possible to check for such a change by looking at Figure 6.3, which shows the relative proportion of no + Verb sentences and don't + Verb sentences for each of the 20 recording sessions.

Figure 6.3 shows a sharp decline in the no + Verb sentences at tape 11. This decline is followed by a sharp increase in the don't + Verb sentences at tape 12. After this, don't + Verb continues to increase at the expense of no + Verb until both forms are equal in number at tape 20. It seems likely, then, that the two halves of the data might best be described by two different variable rules. To test this hypothesis, the data are divided into halves at tape 10 and the program is run on each half. The results are seen in Figures 6.4 and 6.5. The average chi square score for the first half of the data is .630, a reasonably low score. The average chi square score for the second half of the data, however, is higher, .833. This difference might indicate that for the second half of the data there are one or more important constraints not considered.

Figure 6.3 Development of negation in Alberto showing proportion of each negating device to total negatives in each sample.

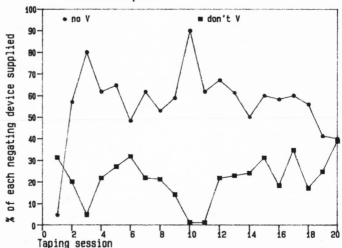

Figure 6.4 Results of the Cedergren-Sankoff program run on data in the first 5-month period.

Subject environment		Verb environment		Complement environment	
I =	.636	like =	.681	∅ =	.710
Other sub.=	.364	MV =	.590	Noun =	.541
		can =	.429	Pronoun =	.417
		have =	.303	Other =	.327

Input = .420; Average chi-square = .630

Figure 6.5 Results of the Cedergren-Sankoff program run on data in the second 5-month period not coded for style constraint.

Subject environment		Verb environment		Complement environment	
I =	.592	can =	.783	Noun =	.661
Other sub.=	.408	MV =	.601	Other =	.513
		like =	.540	Pronoun =	.423
		have =	.136	∅ =	.399

Input = .807; Average chi-square = .833

To supplement his conversational data, Schumann employed an elicitation technique which drew his subject's attention to his way of speaking. Schumann provided a declarative sentence and then asked Alberto to transform it into the negative. It is possible that Alberto was able to monitor[2] his speech in this formal, test-like situation, and therefore produced more negatives with don't. To test this hypothesis we can look to see how often Alberto supplied don't + Verb in the transformational task. During the first half of the sample he supplied don't + Verb 44 percent of the time in this formal situation. In casual conversation don't + Verb was supplied 38 percent of the time. The difference here is not great, and it seems likely that during the first five-month period, monitoring does not greatly constrain the application of rule (3). During the second half of the sample, however, Alberto supplied don't + Verb 82 percent of the time in the translation task compared to 46 percent of the time in casual speech. Clearly, then, at some point monitoring began to constrain rule (3). This conclusion is borne out by the computer program. It is possible to code the computer program for style constraints as well as for linguistic constraints. Coding the second half of the sample to include the environments 'monitored style' and 'unmonitored style', the computer produces the results shown in Figure 6.6.

Figure 6.6   Results of Cedergren-Sankoff program run on data in the second 5-month period coded for style constraint.

Subject environment		Verb environment		Complement environment	
I =	.745	can =	.837	∅ =	.677
Other sub.=	.255	MV =	.491	Noun =	.522
		have =	.343	Other =	.427
		like =	.278	Pronoun =	.342

Input = .807; Average chi-square = .507; monitored style = .893; unmonitored style = .107

Figure 6.6 has an average chi-square of .507, the lowest score so far and well below 1.0 per environment. We can therefore be reasonably certain that Alberto's production of negative sentences during the second five months of the study can be modeled with a variable rule whose constraints are ordered in the same way as the factors in Figure 6.6.

The analysis represented by Figures 6.4 and 6.6 is preferred to the analysis represented by Figures 6.1 and 6.5 because the average chi-square scores of the former are lower. The former analysis appears to make better sense psycholinguistically as well. The ordering of complement constraints from lightest to heaviest is: (1) no complement, (2) noun, (3) pronoun, other complement. This ordering appears to reflect processing complexity. A sentence with no complement should be easier to process than a sentence with a complement. A noun complement should be easier to process than a pronoun since the latter must be declined for case, person, number and gender. The category 'other' should be relatively difficult since it includes embedded sentences, and thus an additional proposition. It is important to note that the psychological claim is for the order of constraints but not for the number assigned to each constraint by the computer program. In other words, variable rules can have psychological reality but not the VARB Rule 2 program, which is just a heuristic device to help the analyst write a variable rule. Thus, a partial variable rule which makes sense psychologically would look like (4).

$$(4)\; S_{Neg} \longrightarrow NP \; + \; \underline{don't} \; + \; Verb \qquad Complement$$

$$\left\langle \begin{array}{c} I \\ Other \\ Subject \end{array} \right\rangle \qquad \left\langle \begin{array}{c} \emptyset \\ Noun \\ Pronoun \\ Other \end{array} \right\rangle$$

As noted above, the claim that constraint ordering can reflect cognitive complexity is compatible with the ZISA group's notion of restrictive simplification. Meisel (1983) observes that sometimes learners simplify structures that have been partially acquired in order to reduce the complexity of the utterance as a whole.

> In second language acquisition... learners do produce utterances that are structurally simplified... although it can be assumed that their transitional competence at this point contains rules that generate the corresponding nonsimplified structures. In other words, a more simplified version of the language is used than what might be expected at a given stage of grammatical development in L2 acquisition. This phenomenon is restrictive simplification (p.127).

Because human language processing capacity is limited, when a learner produces a new, difficult feature, other features in the utterance may be affected. When Alberto desires to express a complex structure, such as an embedded sentence, he tends to backslide in producing the negative structure, producing no instead of don't.

Notice that describing Alberto's use of no + Verb as restrictive simplification involves a slight change in the meaning of that term. Meisel defined restrictive simplification as the omission of an element in order to avoid processing complexity, but the present claim is that backsliding to an earlier form, which perhaps must be a universally simpler form, will also reduce processing complexity and therefore counts as restrictive simplification as well.

In conclusion, Alberto uses restrictive simplification to reduce the overall complexity of an utterance which contains the difficult form don't. The effect of restrictive simplification can be modeled by variable rule (4), which shows that Alberto simplifies more frequently in more complex sentences. Variable rules, then, are useful tools in a psychologically real model of language acquisition.

Notes

1. White's book is an attempt to reconcile the invariant Extended Standard Theory with the facts of variation in language acquisition, and it is approvingly cited by Romaine (1984). But White ends up endorsing a model of language acquisition that is not so different from the one advocated here. In addition to accepting variable rules, she accepts the following propositions which are inconsistent with Chomsky's concept of the ideal speaker-hearer: language acquisition is not instantaneous; different children have different internal grammars; the data

for a theory of acquisition should include not only intuitions about grammaticality but also what children actually say and the results of psychological experiments. Thus, White has departed from the idea that transformational grammar is a formal system whose purpose is to generate all and only the sentences in a language, and whose explanatory adaquacy is measured only by internal evidence. She does not realize that in making this departure she has constructed a theory of performance, not competence.

2. The word monitor is used here in Labov's sense of attention paid to speech, as discussed in Chapter 2, not in Krashen's sense. In Chapter 8 Labov's monitor theory is compared to Krashen's Monitor Model.

Chapter 7

PROTOTYPES AND VARIABLE RULES

In Chapter 6, it was claimed that variable rules have psychological reality because constraints can reflect the articulatory difficulty or the mental processing complexity of a rule. In this chapter, a second kind of psychological interpretation is claimed: constraints can reflect the partial acquisition of an abstract grammatical category. Four studies that support this claim will be reviewed. In one study, William and Theresa Labov (1976) used a variable rule and the VARB Rule 2 program to model the acquisition of a grammatical category. The other three studies were done outside the variation theory framework, but it will be shown how they can be reinterpreted, and perhaps improved, by using variation methodology. In addition, it will be shown how variation theory can be applied to the study of mental prototypes--one of the most robust areas of cognitive psychology.

Unfortunately, none of the four studies reviewed here involves second language learners. This is because, at present, there are no comparable studies on second language acquisition. However, many second language acquisition scholars believe that the basic cognitive processes of first and second language acquisition and use are similar, although at present this is a very controversial position (see Krashen, Scarcella and Long, 1982). For example, Vollmer and Sang (1983:38), in reviewing Oller's influential Unified Competence Hypothesis, note: '[Oller] asserts that all processes of comprehending and producing utterances, of understanding and conveying meaning... are governed by ... one indivisible intellectual force--in L1 as well as in any L2.'

Krashen (1982) is perhaps the most influential scholar whose theory of second language acquisition implies that the basic cognitive processes of first and second language acquisition are very similar. Krashen's theory suggests that the difference in the success rate of first and second language learners is due mainly to affective factors, not cognitive factors. His theory is reviewed in detail in Chapter 8, Section 1.

1. A prototype morphological category. The first study to be reviewed suggests how children acquire and store morphological knowledge. In Chapter 5, we saw that psychologists use schemas to model declarative knowledge and that some kinds of declarative knowledge are intimately connected to sentence productions. Bybee and Slobin (1982) found that schemas may be accessed during the production of irregular past tenses. Investigating how children acquire the past tense forms of verbs, they observed several interesting things, some of which had been noticed before. First, children seem to learn irregular past tense forms by rote, rather than by using the complex, highly abstract rules suggested by generative phonology. Second, children often regularize irregular past forms like <u>ran</u> into forms like <u>runned</u>. This fact suggests that regular past tense forms are learned by rule rather than by rote, since the rule is overextended to irregular verbs. Third, if an irregular verb already ends in a /t/ or /d/, children are less likely to regularize it than if it ends in some other sound. Thus, forms like <u>hitted</u> are rarer than forms like <u>runned</u>. Bybee and Slobin explain that this is because <u>hit</u> already resembles the regular past tense since it ends in an alveolar stop. This evidence suggests that children construct a schema such as (1), which they consult when producing verbs in the past tense.

(1)   A past tense form ends in /t/ or /d/.

Bybee and Slobin tested the psychological reality of (1) by asking children and adults to form the past tense of nonsense words, as in the following task:

This is a girl who knows how to <u>fid</u>. She is <u>fidding</u>. She did the same thing yesterday. What did she do yesterday? Yesterday she ...

Children often supplied forms like <u>fid</u>; adults were much more likely to supply regularized past forms like <u>fidded</u>. Thus, adults were more likely to use the rule for regular past tense, and children were more likely to use a schema such as (1).

In a second study, Bybee and Moder (1983) discovered that children also use schemas to represent irregular past tense forms, as in (2).

(2)   Class II verbs have the past tense form:
       /Λ/ + velar or nasal

Schema (2) says that there is a class of irregular verbs (class II) whose past tense has the vowel /Λ/ and ends in a velar or a nasal. Examples include <u>stung</u> and <u>dug</u>. The problem with schema (2) is that it does not state all the information that Bybee and Moder discovered about class II verbs. For example, (2) does not state that a class II verb is more likely to have both the nasal and velar features rather than just one of them. Nor does (2) state that class II verbs are likely to begin with an /s/ followed by one or more consonants, as in <u>strung</u> and <u>struck</u>.

Bybee and Moder found that class II verbs are defined by their phonological shape. In order to specify this shape more exactly than in (2), they conducted the following experiment. Adult subjects were rapidly read a list of nonsense verbs such as <u>strig</u> and asked to guess what their past tense might be. The subjects sometimes produced a regularized past tense like <u>strigged</u> and sometimes produced a class II past tense like <u>strug</u>. By varying the initial and final consonants and the vowel, Bybee and Moder were able to discover the phonological features of the cue words that were most likely to elicit the class II form. These features are obviously very similar to the phonological features of the past tense forms themselves since the only difference between the cue forms and the elicited past tense forms is that the latter must have the vowel /ʌ/. Some of the cue word features which favored the production of a class II form are shown in Figure 7.1.

Figure 7.1 shows what happens when the initial consonants of the cue word are held constant and the final consonant is changed. The final consonants /ŋ/ and /ŋk/, which have the features velar and nasal, are most likely to elicit the class II form. The effect of the feature velar seems to be slightly stronger than the effect of the feature nasal since the subjects supplied class II forms 25 percent of the time when only velar was present compared to 21 percent of the time when only nasal was present. By holding the final consonants of the cue words constant and changing the initial consonants, Bybee and Moder were able to discover which initial consonants most favored the production of class II forms.

Figure 7.1   The effect of varying the final segment of the cue word on production of irregular past tense forms.

	% responses with /ʌ/
sCCI___:	
Finals: ŋ, nk	44
k, g	25
n, m	21
C	4

Bybee and Moder's experiment shows that their subjects have a more or less clear mental representation of the kind of verb which takes an irregular past form with the vowel /ʌ/. They propose to model this knowledge by means of a prototype schema, instead of schema (2). The prototype, or most typical form class II form, is shown in (3).

(3)   /s/   C   (C)   /ʌ/   /ŋ/

Bybee and Moder speculate that in the experiment, their subjects mentally constructed both a regular past tense form and an irregular past tense form of the cue word. The subjects then compared the irregular form to (3). If the hypothetical irregular form was similar to (3), they uttered it; otherwise, they uttered the regular past tense form.

Prototype schema (3) is more specific than schema (2), but it still does not indicate everything we know about class II forms. For example, (3) does not state that a candidate for membership in the mental category CLASS II VERB must have /ʌ/, but need not have /s/ (though it would be nice). Nor does (3) indicate that a final velar consonant is nicer (more central to the class) than a final nasal consonant. This kind of information, however, did emerge from Bybee and Moder's experiment (they presented it in tables such as Figure 7.1) and therefore, presumably, is contained in the mental representations of speakers.

The linguistic features in Figure 7.1 which favor the production of a
class II past tense form look very much like constraints on a variable
rule, suggesting that the CLASS II VERB prototype could be more
elegantly characterized using variable rule notation, as in (4).

(4)   A class II verb has the past tense form:

$$\Gamma \; (/s/) \; C \; (C) \qquad \begin{array}{c} V \\ \begin{bmatrix} +\text{central} \\ +\text{mid} \end{bmatrix} \end{array} \qquad \begin{array}{c} C \\ \begin{bmatrix} A(+\text{velar}) \\ B(+\text{nasal}) \end{bmatrix} \end{array}$$

Rule (4) specifies the necessary (though not the sufficient) features and
the optional features of the mental prototype CLASS II VERB. The
necessary features are an initial consonant, a midcentral vowel, and a
final consonant. It is unlikely that any class II words would have only
these features (though perhaps cut is an example). The optional features are ranked in the order of their importance, using the Greek
letter notation described in Chapter 2, Section 6. A past tense form
with the alpha and gamma constraints present (such as strug) is closer
to the prototype than a form with the beta and gamma constraints
present (such as strum). The class II verb schema discovered by Bybee
and Moder can thus be written using variable notation.

Bybee and Slobin (1982) suggest that in language acquisition schemas may be the cognitive precursors to categorical rules, so that the
cognitive strategies children use to acquire morphological knowledge
may be ordered as follows: (1) rote learned forms (amalgams), (2) a
schema for relating the rote learned forms, (3) a categorical rule. Let
us examine this acquisition process more closely as it applies to learning the past tense of class II verbs. The child's task is to construct a
prototype schema for the past tense of certain verbs. This is done by
abstracting features from the rote learned forms. Some features must
be marked as essential for class membership (such as $/\Lambda/$), other
features must be marked as only favoring membership (such as initial
/s/). Undoubtedly, universal acquisition strategies aid the child in this
task. For example, Slobin's operating principle (1973:191)[6] pay
attention to the ends of words,' implies that the final velar or nasal will
be more critical than the initial /s/, as indeed it is. However,
universals cannot do the whole job of specifying the schema. Experience must play some role; for example, the fact that a final velar is
more central to the schema than a final nasal can only be acquired
from exposure to English irregular verbs.

Bybee and Slobin speculate that for some linguistic phenomena,
such as the regular past tense, the process of abstracting from amalgams proceeds until the child has isolated the defining features of the
class. At this point the schema can be replaced by a categorical rule,
such as the regular past tense rule for verbs which end in voiceless
sounds, which is similar to the regular plural rule for nouns which end
in voiceless sounds, discussed in Chapter 5, Section 2. However, traces
of the schema remain as a kind of backup system. The existence of
both a rule and a backup schema is suggested by Bybee and Slobin's

experiment where children relied on schema (1) for producing past tenses, but adults usually used the regular past tense rule. The fact that adults did not always use this rule suggests that schema (1) had not disappeared completely.

The regular past tense rule (as well as the regular plural rule) is called a 'source-oriented alteration' because a base form is modified to produce the past tense. In order to construct this rule, the learner must discover a procedure that will apply to all base forms of a class of regular English verbs. Until this procedure has been discovered, regular past tense forms are learned individually and related to each other by means of schema (1). But in the case of the irregular class II verbs, there is no procedure that will produce all members of the class by modifying a base form because there are no defining features of class II verbs. Thus, a schema is the highest level of abstraction possible, and so remains the principle for mentally organizing the class II forms. Since this schema involves only past tense forms, not base forms, it is called a 'product-oriented' schema.

In conclusion, Bybee and Moder's data suggest that some open class grammatical categories, such as the category of class II verbs, lack defining features, and so are mentally represented as prototype schemas. A prototype, in this case, is a bundle of weighted features such as (4) which specifies the central member of the category, and other possible members which do not share all the features of the prototype form. Forms that share only a few features are in the fuzzy border area of the category. Speech performance and grammatical judgments involving these peripheral members will be variable.

2. Prototype syntactic categories. Now consider a prototype explanation for variation in syntax. Transformational-generative grammar assumed that syntactic categories like NP were discrete-- something either was or was not an NP. Furthermore, in general, any NP could participate in all the transformations which took NP in their structural description. Ross (1973) noticed that this assumption was not correct: some NPs, like Harpo or the car, seem to be more nouny than others since they can participate in transformations that other NPs, like existential there and weather it, cannot, as shown in Figure 7.2. Therefore, Ross claimed that membership in a syntactic category is not an all or nothing phenomenon, but--like membership in the morphological category 'class II verb'--is a matter of degree. Thus, in a way, syntactic categories are like prototype schemas. At the center of the NP category are such 'copper-clad, brass bottomed' NPs (Ross 1973:96) as Harpo and the car. These NPs can participate in all transformations calling for NP in their structural description and therefore are like prototype members of the category. But as Figure 7.2 shows, other NPs like there and weather it cannot participate in as many transformations and so are less central members of the category. It is not clear whether central members of the NP category share certain semantic features the way central members of the class-II verb category share phonological features; however, it seems likely that they do. For example, Figure 7.2 suggests that NPs that are concrete and animate can participate in more transformations than other kinds of NPs.

Figure 7.2   The effect of three transformations on a central member and a peripheral member of the Noun Phrase squish.

Type of NP	NP	Transformation	Effect
Central	Harpo	Tag question	Harpo cheated. —→Harpo cheated, didn't he?
		Raising	It will be shown that Harpo cheated. —→Harpo will be shown to have cheated.
		Double raising	It is likely that it will be shown that Harpo cheated. —→ Harpo is likely to be shown to have cheated.
Peripheral	there	Tag question	There were ten files here. —→There were ten files here, weren't there?
		Raising	It will be shown that there were ten files here. —→? There will be shown to have been ten files here.
		Double raising	It is likely that it will be shown that there were ten files here. —→?? There is likely to be shown to have been ten files here.

Ross's work was done before prototype theory became well known, and for awhile it was unclear how the discovery of nondiscrete syntactic categories (which Ross called "squishes") would affect linguistic theory, other than showing that categorical grammar is inadequate. Ross (1974) connected squishes with psycholinguistics by predicting that children would first produce transformed sentences like passives by using words which are central members of a syntactic category. This prediction parallels Rosch's (1973) finding that people learn names for central members of semantic categories more easily than they learn names for more peripheral members.

Ross's prediction was tested by de Villiers (1980), who trained 37 children between the ages of 2.10 and 4.10 from a variety of socio-economic levels to produce passive and cleft sentences. Only the passive experiment is described here, but the results of the cleft sentence experiment were essentially the same. The children, who did not produce passives in their speech, were shown pictures of an animal performing some action that involved an agent and a direct object, such as a frog lifting a rabbit or a tiger smelling a flower. One group of children was trained by imitating the passive sentence which described the picture, for example: 'The frog is being lifted by the rabbit.' On randomly placed trial tests the children were asked to describe the picture, thus (hopefully) eliciting the passive structure. A second group of children was trained by asking them to describe the pictures and then expanding their sentences into passives. These children also were tested by asking them to describe a picture. The pictures were designed to elicit passives that fell into three different groups. Type A passives involved an action verb affecting an animate direct object. De Villiers (1980:26) believed that this kind of sentence 'somehow constitutes a prototype for learning the passive construction.' Type B pictures involved an action verb and an inanimate direct object. Type C pictures involved a nonaction verb and an inanimate object. De Villiers predicted that: (1) children trained on type A events would produce more passives than children trained on type C events; (2) children would produce more type A passives regardless of their training. Both predictions proved correct.

De Villiers found that all groups of children produced more type A passives than other types, and more type B passives than type C passives. The fact that types A and B outranked type C indicates that the children preferred a pattern involving an action verb. The fact that type A outranked types B and C indicates that the children preferred the subject of the passive sentence (which is the logical direct object) to be animate. De Villiers concluded that the syntactic category Verb is mentally represented as a prototype schema with action verbs as the central members. Similarly, the category Subject is organized around animate NPs. Apparently, the animate surface subject was a more important feature of the passive sentence than the action verb.

Translating de Villiers' findings into variation theory terminology, we can say that the children learned a variable rule in which +animate surface subject was the heavier constraint and +action verb was the lighter constraint. This rule would look like (5).

(5) $S_{Passive} \longrightarrow$

$$
\begin{bmatrix} NP \\ +patient \\ A(+animate) \end{bmatrix} + \underline{(is)} + \underline{(being)} \quad \begin{matrix} +Verb +(en) + \underline{(by)} \\ [B(+action)] \end{matrix} \quad \begin{matrix} NP \\ [+agent] \end{matrix}
$$

Rule (5) says that the passive pattern is most likely to be used when: (1) the first NP is animate and (2) the verb is an action verb; next most likely when only (1) is present; least likely when neither (1) nor (2) is present.

We might ask whether the optional elements is, being, en, and by should be marked as constraints in (5). The answer is that they probably should, although lacking de Villiers' data, it is impossible to tell what effect they have. But it seems likely that the children sometimes omitted these morphemes because they used restrictive simplification to reduce processing complexity, as suggested by Meisel (see Chapter 6 of this volume, Section 2).

3. The acquisition of a syntactic category. Now consider a longitudinal study of a child's acquisition of a linguistic category. William and Theresa Labov's (1976) study of how their daughter Jessie acquired Aux + Subject order (inversion) in Wh questions is the most sophisticated use of variation theory to model language acquisition. The Labovs' account is compatible with Ross's theory of a hierarchy of membership within a syntactic category.

The Labovs studied the emergence of Wh questions in their daughter Jessie's speech over a two-year period from the time these forms first appeared until the time they closely resembled adult usage. They particularly focused on subject-verb inversion, which occurs in (7) but not in (6).

(6)   What the address is?
(7)   What is this?

The Labovs discovered that Jessie's first Wh questions included rote forms, as in (8) and (9).

(8)   How 'bout that Mama? (T. Labov dressing J.)
(9)   How 'bout the face? (T. Labov washing J.'s hands. She has just said that she will wash J.'s face).

Here, how 'bout is a general purpose expression. It can be used to initiate a conversation, as in (8), to take a turn in the conversation, as in (9), and (with much help from the physical context) to make a request, as in (10).

(10)   How 'bout these, Mommy? (bringing clothes to T. as T. tries to get J. dressed in them)

About six weeks after (8) was spoken, Jessie coupled how 'bout with a verb, as in (11) and (12).

(11)   How 'bout /də/ cat? (to T. Labov as T. puts food in dog's dish)
(12)   How 'bout get ketchup? (eating french fries, to T.)

The Labovs show that soon after these forms appeared, the rote form how 'bout was expanded to include how come and how do, where do is an invariant, not an analyzed form. They represent these constructions with phrase structure rule (S1).

(S1) $Q_{\overrightarrow{how}}$ how $\left\{ \begin{array}{l} \text{'bout} \\ \text{come} \\ \text{do} \end{array} \right\}$ + NP + (VP)

Rule (S1) produces sentences like (13) and (14).

(13)   How 'bout you move so we both can have some space to lie down?
(14)   How do babies get inside their mommies?

Where and what questions began somewhat later, probably based on analogy with (S1). At first these questions involved only copula-like constructions, although naturally no analyzed copula was involved. Jessie said things like (15) and (16), which were produced by phrase structure rules (S2) and (S3).

(15)   Where Daddy?

(16)   What's that?

(S2) Q_{where} → <u>where (s)</u> + NP

(S3) Q_{what} → <u>what (s)</u> + NP

Although (S2) and (S3) produced the appearance of correct subject-verb order, a productive rule was not involved since the optional /s/ was not analyzed as a tense carrying Aux. Soon, however, Wh questions began to appear which could not have been produced by (S2) and (S3)--for example, (17) and (18).

(17)   What the address is?

(18)   What that means?

Sentences like (17) and (18) are closer to the adult rule since they do carry tense. They might have been produced by a phrase structure rule like (S4).

(S4) Q_{wh} ———→ Wh + NP + Aux + VP

Thus, the variation between the seemingly inverted forms and the uninverted forms was caused by (S4) alternating with the amalgams (S1-3). During this period, Jessie almost never inverted <u>why</u> questions. Therefore, the Labovs suggest that she had no rule for inversion after <u>why</u>. Rather, her rule for <u>why</u> questions was:

(S5) Q_{why} ———→ <u>why</u> + NP + (S)

It is clear that during the early period Aux + Subject order was produced by rules (S1-3) because these forms almost never contained the full copula, only the /s/, which produced the appearance of the contracted copula. However, as time passed, forms which were inverted but not contracted began to appear, such as (19).

(19)   Where is Philadelphia?

These forms could not have been produced by (S1-3) or by (S4), so a productive inversion rule must have been emerging. The Labovs measured the decline of rules (S1-3) in favor of the new rule by using the VARB Rule 2 computer program to determine the effect of contraction as a constraint on inversion. If contraction favored inversion, this would indicate that rules (S1-3) were still being used, since these rules could not produce the uncontracted copula; however, if contraction had no association with inversion, Jessie must be using the new rule. The VARB Rule 2 analysis shows that in January, 1975 contraction highly favored Aux + Subject order, but by July, 1975 contraction had ceased to favor this order. The Labovs concluded that during this period rules (S1-3) coalesced to form a productive variable rule for Aux + Subject order. A simplified version of the variable rule for this order, as analyzed by the VARB Rule 2 program, is shown in (20).

(20) $Q_{wh} \longrightarrow$ Wh-NP   +   Aux +   Subject +   X

$$\left\langle \begin{array}{l} +\text{manner} \\ +\text{locative} \\ +\text{concrete} \\ +\text{temporal} \end{array} \right\rangle$$

Rule (20) says that Aux + Subject word order occurs after the abstract semantic category WH-NP. This category contains members which correspond to the semantic notions in a sentence which a Wh word can question. That is, WH-NP$[_{+\text{manner}}]$ represents the concept of questioning the manner in which something was done. WH-NP$[_{+\text{concrete}}]$ represents questioning the receiver of an action, that is, (the direct object), and so on. The Labovs account for the constraint ordering in (20) by observing that the semantic notions these constraints represent are ordered independently in the grammar according to their 'degree of integration' into a sentence. That is, the notion 'receiver of action' (direct object) is more integrated into its proposition than the notion 'time of action' (as noted in Chapter 3), and so on. Ross (1981) agrees with the Labovs' explanation, saying, in effect, that the category WH-NP is a squish, some of whose members can participate in more transformations than other members. He notes that the relative centrality of the members of WH-NP is reflected in their order of occurrence in a sentence, as in (21).

(21)   He took **the train**   **downtown**   **in a hurry**   **last Wednesday**
             +concrete   +locative   +manner   +time

      for a very good reason.
      +reason

In (21) the constituent which is closest to the verb (+ concrete) is the most integrated into the sentence. At the other end of the scale, the constituent which is farthest from the verb (+reason) is the least integrated into the sentence. Ross (1981) cites five additional syntactic phenomena which support the idea that the ordering of constraints in (20) more or less (we will get to less in a minute) reflects the degree to which these notions are integrated into a sentence. One of his arguments (Ross 1981:243) is as follows:

For me, the higher the degree of integration a constituent exhibits, the less easy it is to have a free-standing one-word question.

A: Ted must be off painting.

B: $\left\{ \begin{array}{l} \text{Why} \\ \text{Where?} \\ \text{?How} \\ \text{*What} \end{array} \right\}$

Thus, the notion of reason can be questioned by a sentence of a single word, but the notions of direct object and of manner resist being pulled out of a proposition and represented by a single word.

To summarize the Labovs' and Ross's account, from individually learned phrase structure rules similar to (S1-3), Jessie constructed the mental category WH-NP. The members of this category were the four abstract notions of questioning a sentence constituent, namely questioning manner, location, direct object, and time. Some of these notions were more central to the WH-NP category, and therefore in sentences involving these notions Jessie was more likely to employ rule (20). Thus, Jessie's use of rule (20) was like de Villiers' subjects' use of rule (5). Those subjects employed (5) more often when a central member of the category Subject was present and when a central member of the category Verb was present.

There are some possible problems with the Labovs' and Ross's account. One problem is the claim that very abstract notions like NP-WH $_{+locative}$ figure in syntactic rules. Since the Labovs wrote their paper in 1976, the trend in linguistics and psycholinguistics has been toward writing linguistic rules that are closer to surface structure. A second problem is that the order of constraints in (20) and the order predicted by (21) and the other syntactic arguments don't match. Jessie's constraint ordering is shown in (22a) and the degree of integration scale is shown in (22b) (for convenience, Wh words are used to represent the abstract notions like WH-NP +locative.

(22a)	(22b)
how	what
where	where
what	how
when	when
why	why

The Labovs explain the discrepency involving how by pointing to its different developmental history; the phrase structure rule (S1) which produced how questions is different from phrase structure rules (S2) and (S3) which produced what and where questions. For one thing, rule (S1) does not just question the manner in which something is done, although it can be used to question this notion, using how + do. But the rule also generates how + come, which seems to question reason, and how + 'bout, which may still be used as a general purpose expression as in (8) and (9). Therefore, how is out of consideration. The remaining discrepency involves what, which should change places with where, if Jessie's constraint ordering is to match the degree of integration ordering. The Labovs explain, however, that the frequency of Aux + Subject order was really about the same after what and where, so these constraints should be weighted about equally. Thus, the constraint ordering: (1) where, what (2) when does reflect the integration of these notions into the proposition. This reasoning also explains the behavior of why. Why does not participate in rule (2) because it represents the notion least integrated into the proposition.

A different, though perhaps compatible, explanation for Jessie's constraint ordering is shown in variable rule (23). Rule (23) claims that Aux + Subject order is constrained by the actual lexical items how, what, where, and when, rather than by the semantic notions these words question. This rule has the advantage of being less abstract than

(20) and also of accounting for how.

(23) $Q_{wh} \longrightarrow$ Wh word + Aux + Subject + X
$$\left\langle \begin{array}{c} \text{how} \\ \text{where} \\ \text{what} \\ \text{when} \end{array} \right\rangle$$

Rule (23) represents a coalescing of rules (S1-3). It claims that Jessie is 'realizing' that when how, where, what, and when begin a sentence, Aux precedes Subject. The various Wh words are related by means of a prototype schema, in which some words are more central than others. The degree of centrality is explained not by reference to the semantic notions the words question, but by the order in which the rules (S1-3) were learned.

Perhaps a good way to think about a prototype syntactic category schema, like Wh Word in (23), is suggested by Hatch (1983), who says that learners 'pencil in' hypotheses about the language they are acquiring. If these hypotheses are supported by intake, the penciling becomes darker. In the Wh Word schema, how is darker than where, and so on, because how has been used as a question word longer than where, and where longer than when, etc.

The Wh Word schema might function in the production process in the same way that the class II past tense schema does. Recall that Bybee and Slobin (1982) speculated that in constructing a past tense form, the speaker has available both the regularized form and the irregular form. If the irregular form is not too different from the class II prototype, it is likely to be produced because it will 'sound right' at an abstract level. Perhaps Wh questions are produced in the same way. Chapter 5, Section 4, reviewed evidence that sentences are planned not word by word but clause by clause. Perhaps the speaker has available an abstract representation of a clause in both the Aux + Subject order and Subject + Aux order. If the first word in the clause is a central member of the Wh Word category, the Aux + Subject form will 'sound right,' and will be produced. In other words, when producing Wh questions a speaker must choose between two syntactic plans. The plan modeled by rule (23) is chosen more often when the Wh word is one which is central to the Wh Word category.

Notice that Jessie's mental analysis of Wh words goes through the same three stages described by Bybee and Slobin: (1) rote learned forms, (2) a schema for relating the rote learned forms, (3) a categorical rule. In the first stage, the individual Wh words are not associated--they are part of separate phrase structure rules. In the third stage, the different words are analyzed as full-fledged members of the Wh word category. The second stage is the transitional period. In it, the various Wh words are loosely associated by means of a schema, with some of the words more central to the schema than others. This transitional period can be modeled by a variable rule in which the various Wh words act as more or less powerful constraints.

4. A prototype semantic category. As a final example of the relationship between variation theory and prototype theory, we consider a study in semantics. Coleman and Kay (1981) claim that the semantic representation of the word lie (prevaricate) consists of a prototype which includes three basic features:

(24a) The speaker believes the statement to be false.
(24b) The speaker intends to deceive the listener.
(24c) The statement is in fact false.

Coleman and Kay created eight different stories, each of which contained a possible lie with a different combination of the three features. For example, story (L1) contains a lie with all three features.

(L1)   Moe has eaten the cake Juliet was intending to serve to company. Juliet asks Moe, 'Did you eat the cake?' Moe says, 'No.' Did Moe lie?

Story (L2) contains an example of a 'social lie' with only features (22a) and (24c).

(L2)   Schmallowitz is invited to dinner at his boss's house. After a dismal evening enjoyed by no one, Schmallowitz says to his hostess, 'Thanks, it was a terrific party'... Did Schmallowitz lie?

Coleman and Kay asked 67 subjects to rate the possible lies in the stories on a seven-point scale where a rating of 7.0 indicated that the subject was 'very sure it was a lie', and a rating of 1.0 indicated that the subject was 'very sure it was not a lie'. Coleman and Kay assumed that story (L1) contained a prototype lie, and therefore predicted that it would receive the highest rating, and that the ratings of the other stories would correspond to how well their lies matched the prototype. Coleman and Kay then ranked the stories by using a mean scale score. As they predicted, story (L1) got the highest rating (6.96), and the other stories were judged to contain lies to the degree that the possible lies diverged from the prototype.

Figure 7.3   Cross-products chart ranking features of the prototype lie

Features Believe to be false	intent to deceive	false in fact	mean scale score	story number
		+	6.96	1
+	+			
		-	5.16	4
	-	+	4.70	5
		-	4.61	8
	+	+	3.66	3
-		-	3.48	6
	-	+	2.97	7
		-	1.06	2

Coleman and Kay then showed that the features of lie were not weighted equally by using the equivalent of a cross-products chart, such as the one in Figure 7.3, which shows that the features of lie are weighted in the order in (24a-24c).The fact that the cross-products chart in Figure 7.3 fits the data ('scales') perfectly, indicates that the effect of one feature is independent of the effects of other features-- that is, there is no interaction of features. As we have seen, this is usually the case with constraints on a phonological or syntactic rule.

Coleman and Kay concluded that the meaning of lie is mentally represented as a prototype schema, whose internal structure contains weighted features.

5. Conclusion. The world presents us with great variety. Some things in the world are concrete like birds and cups, others are abstract like irregular verbs and lies. Our minds impose order on this teeming mass by generalizing both concrete and abstract things into categories. Sometimes the category members share defining features: brothers are the male children of the same parents. Sometimes the categories are fuzzy and blend into other categories--a cup does not differ from a bowl in any single feature (Labov, 1973). Prototype theory claims that we abstract from our experience of many cups a prototype cup, and when we encounter a cup-like object, we compare it to this prototype. We perceive vessels to be cups to the extent that their features resemble the prototype. If we are asked to classify an object we are not sure about, our judgments vary. Rosch (1973) showed that natural categories can be mentally organized around a prototype. Bybee and Slobin (1982) and Bybee and Moder (1983) showed that abstract linguistic categories can be organized in this way as well. The language acquisition studies by de Villiers (1980) and the Labovs (1976) suggest that children construct prototype schemas as a means of mentally organizing rote learned forms. Often these schemas develop into classical categories with clear boundries, which can serve as the input to categorical rules. Variation theory provides a way of modeling this development.

Chapter 8

VARIATION THEORY AND THE MONITOR MODEL

1. Krashen's theory of monitoring. What are the most effective ESL classroom activities? Steven Krashen (1981, 1982) proposes a way of judging the effectiveness of classroom activities based on a psycholinguistic theory called the Monitor Model. Stevick (1981:270) has called the central claim of this model 'potentially the most fruitful concept for language teachers to come out of the linguistic sciences during my professional lifetime.' Krashen divides classroom activities into two kinds: acquisition activities and learning activities. Acquisition activities expose the student to comprehensible samples of the target language. They include playing games, listening to lectures, responding to commands, reading comprehensible materials, and so on. Learning activities, on the other hand, focus on a particular language form, like tag questions or the phoneme /a/. Learning activities include error correction, mechanical drills, and grammar explanations. Acquisition activities might be engaged in by someone acquiring a language naturally, without a teacher. Learning activities, however, require a teacher and often a textbook. The Monitor Model claims that learning activities are only marginally helpful to the student. Acquisition activities are the basic mechanism of internalizing the language.

Before describing the Monitor Model in detail, let us examine the evidence that supports it. Krashen finds indirect support for his model in many areas of second language research, but the best evidence comes from the morpheme acquisition studies such as Dulay and Burt (1974) and Bailey, Madden, and Krashen (1974), which were described in Chapter 1. Recall that these studies found that the order of difficulty of certain English morphemes was about the same for speakers of languages as different as Chinese and Spanish. In a subsequent morpheme study, however, Larsen-Freeman (1975), discovered some possible counterevidence to the universal order of difficulty hypothesis. On one of her tests, she discovered a different order of morpheme difficulty than the order found by the previous researchers. To explain this discrepancy, Krashen looked at the elicitation instruments used by the different researchers. Dulay and Burt (1974) and Bailey, Madden, and Krashen (1974) elicited their data with the Bilingual Syntax Measure (BSM), which requires subjects to answer questions orally about a series of pictures, and thus elicits relatively spontaneous and natural speech. Larsen-Freeman, on the other hand, used a paper and pencil grammar test, in which, for example, the subjects had to fill in the blanks in a story context. Krashen speculates that the two kinds of elicitation tasks tap two different linguistic abilities: the BSM taps basic linguistic competence,[1] but the paper and pencil test, where the subject has plenty of time to think about the correct answer, taps a grammatical problem-solving ability. He suggests that these two abilities stem from separate internal systems of linguistic rules, which can interact in the following way: when there is enough time, the conscious, 'problem-solving' rules can impose themselves on the unconscious basic competence rules and alter what the subject says or writes. This situation is illustrated in Figure 8.1.

Figure 8.1   Basic version of the Monitor Model.

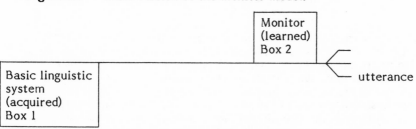

According to the Monitor Model in Figure 8.1, all second language performance is initiated by the basic rules of competence found in box 1 (except in the very early stages, when speakers may laboriously plan an utterance using the problem-solving rules in box 2, which is called the 'Monitor'). In later stages of second language performance, the rules in the Monitor box are used only to modify the basic language structures produced in the competence box. Thus, a subject might have no rule for third person singular -s in box 1 and would therefore never produce this morpheme in speech. However, the subject might have this rule in box 2, and so would be able to produce the form on a paper and pencil grammar test. The Monitor rules can only be used when there is enough time to stop and figure out the correct form. They cannot be used in speech, except perhaps when the first sentence of a discourse is planned out in advance.

Krashen suggests that linguistic knowledge gets into boxes 1 and 2 in entirely different ways. Basic linguistic competence is 'acquired' through exposure to a second language in meaningful contexts. Monitoring ability is 'learned' through error correction, drill, grammatical explanation, and so on. Furthermore, only a particular kind of rule can be learned, namely, a rule that is easy to remember and to apply. Subject-verb agreement is one example. Many linguistic rules, however, are so complicated that they are unlearnable--for example, the rules governing English prepositions. These rules must be acquired.

Although Krashen's evidence for the Monitor Model is indirect and far from conclusive (see Munsell and Carr 1981 for a review), the model is intuitively attractive. It suggests that second language acquisition is basically similar to first language acquisition and that, given motivation and freedom from fear of making errors, adults--like children--can acquire a language naturally and enjoyably. The Monitor Model emphasizes meaningful language use, not artificial and awkward exercises and drills. But before the Monitor Model is accepted, it should be compared to Labov's (1978) idea of monitoring which was discussed in Chapter 2, Section 2.

Krashen (1978c:3) states that his idea of monitoring came from Labov's work, and he suggests that monitoring works similarly in a first or a second language. Like Krashen, Labov developed his theory of monitoring after observing variation in linguistic performance. As was seen in Chapter 2, Black English speakers sometimes produce Black English forms, as in (1), and sometimes Standard English forms, as in (2).

(1) He be late every day.
(2) He is late every day.

Like Krashen, Labov correlated different linguistic forms with different elicitation tasks. Thus, (2) would be more likely in a formal situation where the speaker is paying attention to the form of speech, and (1) would be more likely in an informal situation. Labov theorized that when speakers pay more attention to the form of their speech, they are able to shift their style of speaking to a more formal one. Labov called style shifting in the direction of more 'correct' speech monitoring. An example we have discussed is New Yorkers' use of /r/ following a vowel, described in Figure 2.1.

2. Monitoring and language change. Labov (1972) suggests that monitoring is involved in one of the two basic mechanisms of historical language change. 'Change from below' (meaning change from below the level of consciousness) is unaffected by monitoring. This kind of change usually starts in the lower middle socioeconomic classes. An example is the change, discussed in Chapter 3, Section 6, that occurred on Martha's Vineyard after World War II, when a pronunciation that had almost died out was revived. In 1933, only the oldest residents of Martha's Vineyard used centralized diphthongs--originally a Scottish pronunciation--where, for example, about the house is pronounced /əbəwtǰə həws/. But since the 1940s, young Vineyarders who wished to maintain their identity in the face of tourist invasions from the mainland each summer unconsciously adopted this distinctive pronunciation.

The second mechanism of language change, 'change from above' (meaning change from above the level of consciousness), does involve monitoring. Such change originates in the upper socioeconomic classes and spreads downward, as in the spread of postvocalic /r/ in New York City English. In Chapter 2, we saw how this change originates in a speaker's most monitored style and spreads to other styles. The implication for second language acquisition is that a new linguistic form might begin as a consciously learned rule, used only in a monitored style, and then spread to the less monitored styles. Dickerson (1975) was the first variationist to suggest that second language acquisition might proceed in this way. Her evidence (reviewed in Chapter 6,

Section 2) was that Japanese speakers exhibited style stratification in their pronunciation of the English phoneme /ð/ and that as time passed, their accurate pronuciation appeared to spread from more monitored to less monitored styles.

Tarone (1984, 1985) observed that interlanguage, like first language, varies according to the elicitation task. She cites M. Schmidt's (1980) data, which show that learners from several native language backgrounds were better able to produce sentences with verb ellipsis, as in (3), in contexts which gave them a better chance to monitor.

(3)   Mary is eating an apple and Sue ∅ a pear.

These learners, who never uttered such sentences in free oral speech, were able to produce successively more verb ellipsis in tasks involving elicited imitation (11%), written sentence combining (25%), and grammatical judgment (50%).

Schmidt's and Dickerson's second language subjects appear to be style shifting. Like Labov's New York City informants, their language in more monitored styles is more 'correct' than that in less monitored styles. These results suggest that 'change from above' may be one mechanism of change in second language acquisition. On the basis of these and similar studies, Tarone (1983:146, 158) tentatively concludes:

> The more careful style ... may contain more target language forms ... The more casual style may contain structures ... which occur in pidgins, in early child language acquisition, and early untutored second-language acquisition.

> Structures may first be incorporated into the careful style and over time move along the continuum until they are incorporated into the vernacular style. In Krashen's terms... learned structures may become acquired.

3. Krashen's model versus Labov's model. Can learning become acquisition? Which monitor model is better? A major difference between Labov's monitor model and Krashen's is that for Krashen monitoring is a conscious 'problem solving' process, but for Labov monitoring is sometimes conscious, as when speakers read a list of minimal pairs, and sometimes unconscious, a 'feel for correctness', as when speakers talk in a formal situation. This second kind of monitoring is what happens in the careful speech style of Figure 2.1, where speakers have little time to think about how to pronounce a particular word, yet do manage to supply more /r/s than in their casual speech.

In fact, Labov's model implies that it is impossible to draw the line between conscious and unconscious monitoring. In the 'reading style' of Figure 2.1, for example, some altering of form in the direction of 'correctness' takes place, but is it conscious or unconscious? There is no clear demarcation between the conscious 'problem-solving' kind of monitoring and the unconscious 'feel for correctness' kind. In Labov's model, monitoring is not like an on-off switch; rather, as Stevick (1980:272) points out, it is like a rheostat that can be turned up or down. Labov's definition of monitoring, 'attention paid to the form of speech', seems to describe this phenomenon very well. One can pay more or less attention to form, depending on the circumstances. Smith

(1982:43) describes this situation as follows:

> The word <u>attention</u> ... sometimes implies conscious knowledge and sometimes not ... Attention simply means a kind of orientation, concentration, or focus. If we successfully drive our car we have presumably "attended" to that action, we were focused upon it, but not in the sense that we were consciously aware of what we were doing. If we are engrossed in what we are doing, it is only afterwards that we can remove ourselves from the situation and say what we have done.

If Krashen's model allowed only for altering the form of speech on the basis of conscious monitoring, it would be incomplete, for second language speakers report that they can alter form on the basis of a 'feel for correctness'. Krashen calls this phenomenon 'monitoring' (with a small <u>m</u>), as opposed to 'Monitoring' (with a large <u>M</u>). Thus, monitoring is an unconscious altering of linguistic form in the direction of correctness; it is presumably acquired, not learned. The addition of monitoring to Krashen's theory requires that Figure 8.1 be amended to include a <u>m</u>onitor box, as shown in Figure 8.2.

Figure 8.2   The Monitor Model expanded to account for unconscious monitoring.

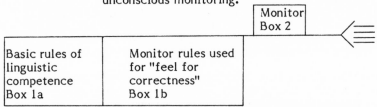

Basic rules of linguistic competence Box 1a	Monitor rules used for "feel for correctness" Box 1b	Monitor Box 2

But the distinction between Monitoring and monitoring seems unnatural, because it requires speakers to carry around in their heads two sets of linguistic rules which can never merge, and also because it implies that monitoring in a second language is completely different from monitoring in a first language.

Having expanded Krashen's model to account for the 'feel for correctness' phenomenon, we consider whether the variation theory model needs to be expanded as well. The studies on monitoring in the native language reviewed so far suggest that the more monitored speech styles contain more 'correct' forms. Perhaps this fact is one reason for Tarone's suggestion that in interlanguage, the more careful style may contain more target language forms. But actually, monitoring by native speakers does not guarantee more 'correct' forms; monitoring can also result in 'structural hypercorrection', where a high prestige form is produced in an inappropriate environment. For example, in monitored speech, Black English speakers whose basic linguistic system does not include third person -<u>s</u> sometimes produce this suffix in the wrong environment, resulting in sentences like <u>We goes to school</u>, or <u>They get caughts</u> (Wolfram and Fasold 1974:156). In other words, it appears that in native speaker speech monitoring is only helpful for forms that are fairly well integrated into the speaker's internal grammar. Structural hypercorrection occurs when 'an overtly favored feature is not thoroughly under control of the speaker' (Wolfram and Fasold 1974:88). These features 'are produced by guesswork and not by rule' (p. 156). It may be that monitoring in a second language, like monitoring in a first language, is only helpful for structures that are fairly well integrated into the speaker's internal grammar. Two recent studies suggest that this is the case.

Tarone (1985) tested the hypothesis that interlanguage elicited in monitored styles is more accurate than that elicited in other styles. Her subjects were from two language groups: ten Arabic speakers and ten Japanese speakers. Only representative data from the Arabic speakers are considered here, but the Japanese speakers' data are comparable. Tarone administered three elicitation tasks: (1) a multiple choice test, (2) an interview, (3) a spoken narrative. Three of the linguistic forms she examined were: third person -s, plural s, and article. The results of Tarone's experiment are shown in Figure 8.3.

Figure 8.3 Style shifting on three target language forms by Arabic speakers.

Morpheme	Elicitation task: Test	Interview	Narrative	Result of monitoring
3rd person -s	67	51	39	Improves accuracy
Noun plural	70	83	71	No change
Article	58	85	91	Decreases accuracy

Numerals indicate percentage correct.

The most obvious conclusion to be drawn from these data is that monitoring is a dangerous tool: in one case out of the three, third person singular -s, monitoring did increase accuracy, but in another case, articles, monitoring decreased accuracy. Clearly, the hypothesis that monitoring always improves accuracy is not supported.

In a similar study of monitoring, Ciske (1984) elicited four contextual styles of English from a Korean student, Kim, who was enrolled in my class in freshman composition for foreign students. Kim was asked to respond to the question, 'How does the U.S. differ from what you had expected?' in four ways: free writing, reading the free writing sample, conversation, and correcting the free writing sample. Ciske then scored the various speech and writing samples for accuracy in obligatory contexts of subject-verb agreement, regular past tense, and prepositions. The results are displayed in Figure 8.4.

The contextual styles in Figure 8.4 are ordered from least to most monitored along the horizontal axis. The order is: free writing, reading the free writing sample, conversation, editing the free writing sample. Obviously, the edited written style is the most monitored, but what is the justification for the rest of the ordering? It has often been observed (for example, by Bartholomae 1980) that second language and second dialect speakers are able to monitor what they have written by reading it aloud. Thus, reading a free writing sample is more monitored than writing it. For many learners, conversation, even with a relative stranger and with a tape recorder present, may be a less monitored style than free writing, but I do not think that this was the case for Kim. Kim had been trained in free writing throughout a semester and had learned very well to ignore form in favor of content in this kind of exercise. Also, he did not expect that his free writing would be marked for accuracy. But in the conversational style Ciske reports (personal communication) that Kim 'definitely wanted to impress me. He often stopped and self-corrected.' Thus, I think that the ordering of contextual styles in Figure 8.4 is correct for this subject. The greatest changes in the accuracy of Kim's English occur between the speaking style and the edited writing style. By monitoring Kim was able to improve significantly the accuracy of subject-verb agreement ($p < .01$) and regular past tense ($p < .001$). On the other hand, the accuracy of preposition usage is significantly lower in the more monitored style ($p < .05$). Ciske's results, then, are similar to Tarone's: sometimes monitoring increases accuracy, but sometimes it decreases accuracy.

Figure 8.4   Monitoring by Kim in four styles.

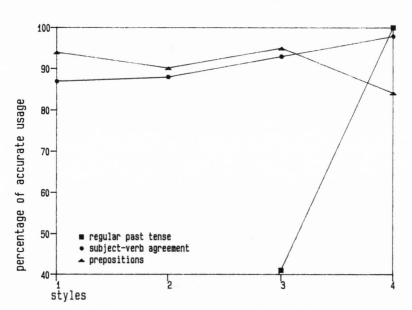

Key: style 1 = free writing; style 2 = reading the free writing; style 3 = interview; style 4 = editing the free writing.

4. The bootstrap hypothesis. Tarone's and Ciske's results suggest a revised version of the monitor model, one that incorporates both Krashen's and Labov's insights. The model, called the 'bootstrap hypothesis', says that if the form being monitored is not in the speaker's basic linguistic competence, monitoring produces structural hypercorrection, thereby decreasing accuracy. However, if the form being monitored is within the speaker's basic competence, monitoring can improve accuracy, especially if the form is 'learnable' in Krashen's sense. If the form is within the speaker's basic competence, but is not learnable, monitoring will decrease accuracy. Thus, the effect of monitoring is determined by two factors: (1) The form must be in the speaker's basic competence; or, more technically, the speaker must have a variable rule that produces the form in obligatory contexts at a fairly high frequency. If factor (1) is present, factor (2) comes into play: (2) The form must be learnable. These factors can be present to varying degrees. The bootstraps hypothesis predicts that when both factors are largely present, monitoring will improve performance and learning can 'pull up' acquisition. However, when both factors are largely absent, monitoring will decrease accuracy and learning will not affect acquisition.

The bootstrap hypothesis accounts for Tarone's and Ciske's data in the following way: in both studies, factor 1 (variable production of the morpheme) was present. Both the Arabic speakers and Kim had some control over the structures in question. Thus, factor 2, learnability, is the crucial factor. The two morphemes whose accuracy was improved by monitoring, subject-verb agreement and third person -s (a kind of subject-verb agreement), are classic examples of 'learnable' structures. On the other hand, the two morphemes whose accuracy was brought down by monitoring (articles and prepositions) are classic examples of 'unlearnable' structures. It is true that monitoring did not improve the accuracy of plural -s, but the bootstrap hypothesis only claims that the presence of factors (1) and (2) is necessary for successful monitoring, not that it is sufficient.

The bootstrap hypothesis, if correct, has several implications for language teaching. The first implication is that learning activities can sometimes be helpful to language acquisition. The value of learning activities, however, will be determined by the extent to which factors (1) and (2) are present. It is especially important that factor (1) be present--that the student already have some control over the structure to be taught. A grammar syllabus, then, cannot be constructed in the abstract; it must emerge from the students themselves. A good technique for deciding which grammar forms to focus on is to notice which forms the students use both correctly and incorrectly in their speech and writing, that is, which forms are variably produced.

A second implication for teaching is that the social situation of speaking will affect students' accuracy. For example, a conversation class will tend to elicit a more monitored style than casual speech, which will improve the accuracy of some structures and decrease the accuracy of others. The teacher must be aware that structural hyper-correction can occur, and understand why students may have particular difficulty trying to monitor for a form that is beyond their basic competence or is unlearnable. Error correction should be confined to structures that the student can monitor for.

A third implication for teaching is that to some extent students can be taught when to depend on the monitor and when not to. For example, it was helpful to Kim for me to point out that when editing a paper he should attempt to correct subject-verb agreement, but leave prepositions alone. A good exercise for helping students gauge their ability to monitor is to ask them to freewrite, as Kim did, paying no attention to form, and then to edit their own writing. Usually, the editing produces changes for the better and for the worse in about equal numbers. The teacher can then go over the paper, pointing out which corrections helped and which did not. After several of these exercises, students can usually edit more effectively.

The judicious use of learning activities may help students become, in Krashen's phrase, 'optimal monitor users'. But monitoring has its dangers. Krashen points out that monitor overusers are insecure about their speech, and therefore hesitant and sometimes even paralyzed. Linguistic insecurity occurs among native speakers as well. Labov (1978:25) observes that 'The norms for pronouncing vase and aunt are now shifting, so that many people are baffled and embarrassed when they encounter these words in a text to be read aloud.' Similarly, if students are corrected too often, they will become embarrassed and finally silent.

Although it seems possible to improve Krashen's Monitor Model, note that Krashen's basic insight, the learning-acquisition distinction, is still most important. Learning activities, though helpful, are not essential, and are still very much secondary to acquisition activities. Perhaps a good rule of thumb for the learning/acquisition mix is one suggested by Paulston and Bruder (1976) in a slightly different context: learning activities should be both present and brief.

Note

1. Competence is used here in its everyday English sense and not in Chomsky's technical sense (see Chapter 5, Section 1).

REFERENCES

Adamson, H.D., and Ceil Kovac. 1981. Variation theory and second language acquisition. In: Variation omnibus. Edited by David Sankoff and Henrietta Cedergren. Carbondale, Ill.: Linguistic Research Inc. 215-25.

Anderson, J.R. 1980. Cognitive psychology and its implications. San Francisco: W.H. Freeman.

Anderson, Roger. 1977. The impoverished state of cross sectional morpheme acquisition/accuracy methodology. Working Papers on Bilingualism 14: 47-82.

Anderson, Roger. 1981a. Two perspectives on pidginization as second language acquisition. In: R. Anderson (1981b:165-95).

Anderson, Roger, ed. 1981b. New dimensions in second language acquisition. Rowley, Mass.: Newbury House.

Anderson, Roger, ed. 1983. Pidginization and creolization as language acquisition. Rowley, Mass.: Newbury House.

Bailey, N., C. Madden, and S. Krashen. 1974. Is there a 'natural sequence' in adult second language learning? Language Learning 21.235-43.

Bartholomae, D. 1980. The study of error. College Composition 31.253-69.

Beebe, Leslie. 1980. Sociolinguistic variation and style shifting in second language acquisition. Language Learning 30.433-45.

Berko, Jean. 1958. The child's learning of English morphology. Word 14.150-77.

Bickerton, Derek. 1977. Pidginization and creolization: Language acquisition and language universals. In: Valdman (1977:49-69).

Bickerton, Derek. 1981. Roots of language. Ann Arbor, Mich.: Korama Publishers.

Bickerton, Derek, and C. Odo. 1976. General phonology and pidgin syntax. Vol. 2 of Final Report on National Science Foundation grant no. GS-39748.

Bower, G.H., J.B. Black, and T. Turner. 1979. Scripts in memory for text. Cognitive Psychology 11.177-220.

Bresnan, Joan. 1978. A realistic transformational grammar. In: Linguistic theory and psychological reality. Edited by M. Halle, J. Bresnan, and G. Miller. Cambridge, Mass.: MIT Press.

Brown, Roger. 1973. A first language: The early stages. Cambridge, Mass.: Harvard University Press.

Bybee, Joan, and C.L. Moder. 1983. Morphological classes as natural categories. Lg. 59.251-69.

Bybee, Joan, and D.I Slobin. 1982. Rules and schemas in the development and use of the English past. Lg. 58.265-89.

Cazden, Courtney, and Roger Brown. 1975. The early development of the mother tongue. In: Foundations of language development: A multidisciplinary approach, vol. 1. Edited by E.H. Lenneberg and E. Lenneberg. New York: Academic Press. 299-310.

Cazden, Courtney, Ellen Rosansky, John Schumann, and Herlinda Cancino. 1975. Second language acquisition sequence in children, adolescents, and adults. Cambridge, Mass: Harvard University Graduate School of Education.

Cedergren, Henrietta, and David Sankoff. 1974. Variable rules: Performance as a statistical reflection of competence. Lg. 50.333-55.

Chomsky, Noam. 1959. Review of: Verbal behavior, by B.F. Skinner. Lg. 35,26-58.

Chomsky, Noam. 1965. Aspects of the theory of syntax. Cambridge, Mass.: MIT Press.

Ciske, Mary. 1984. The monitor model: More evidence. In: WATESOL Working Papers. Edited by Christine Meloni and George Spanos. Washington, D.C.: WATESOL.

Coleman, M., and Paul Kay. 1981. Prototype semantics: The English word lie. Lg. 57.27-44.

Corder, S. Pit. 1977. Language continua and the interlanguage hypothesis. In: Actes du 5eme colloque: Theoretical models in applied linguistics, Universite de Berne, May 31-June 3. 11-17.

Corder, S. Pit. 1981. Formal simplicity and functional simplification. In: R. Anderson (1981b).

de Villiers, Jill. 1980. The process of rule learning in a child's speech: A new look. In: Children's language, vol. 2. Edited by K. Nelson. New York: Gardner Press.

de Villiers, Jill, and Peter de Villiers. 1973. A cross sectional study of the acquisition of grammatical morphemes in child speech. Journal of Psycholinguistic Research 2.267-78.

Dickerson, Lonna. 1975. The learner's interlanguage as a system of variable rules. TESOL Quarterly 9.401-07.

Dreyfus, Hubert. 1972. What computers can't do. New York: Harper and Row.

Dulay, Heidi, and Marina Burt. 1974. Natural sequences in child second language and acquisition. Language Learning 24.37-53.

Fasold, Ralph. 1972. Tense marking in black English: A linguistic and social analysis. Washington,D.C.: Center for Applied Linguistics.

Fathman, Ann. 1975. Language background, age and the order of acquisition of English structures. In: New directions in second language learning, teaching, and bilingual education. Edited by Marina Burt and Heidi Dulay. Washington, D.C.: TESOL. 33-43.

Ferguson, Charles, and C.E. DeBose. 1977. Simplified registers, broken language and pidginization. In: Valdman (1977:99-128).

Fillmore, Charles. 1979. On fluency. In: Individual differences in language ability and language behavior. Edited by Charles Fillmore, D. Kempler, and W.S.-Y. Wang. New York: Academic Press. 85-102.

Fodor, Jerry A., Thomas G. Bever, and Merril F. Garrett. 1974. The psychology of language. New York: McGraw-Hill.

Hamburger, Henry, and Stephen Crain. 1984. Acquisition of cognitive compilation. Cognition 17.85-136.

Hatch, Evelyn. 1983. Psycholinguistics: A second language perspective. Rowley, Mass.: Newbury House.

Huebner, Thom. 1983. A longitudinal analysis of the acquisition of English. Ann Arbor, Mich.: Karoma Publishers.

Hyltenstam, Kenneth. 1977. Implicational patterns in interlanguage syntax variation. Language Learning 27.383-411.

Kay, Paul. 1978. Variable rules, community grammar and linguistic change. In: Linguistic variation: Models and methods. Edited by David Sankoff. New York: Academic Press. 71-84.

Kay, Paul, and Gillian Sankoff. 1974. A language universals approach to pidgins and creoles. In: Pidgins and creoles: Current trends and prospects. Edited by David DeCamp and Ian Hancock. Washington, D.C.: Georgetown University Press. 61-72.

Kay, Paul, and Chad K. McDaniel. 1979. On the logic of variable rules. Language in Society 8.151-87.

Kay, Paul, and Chad K. McDaniel. 1981. On the meaning of variable rules: Discussion. Language in Society 10.251-58.

Keenan, Elinor L., and Bernard Comrie. 1977. Noun phrase accessibility and universal grammar. Linguistic Inquiry 8.63-99.

Kelly, J.P. 1982. Interlanguage variation and social/psychological influences within a developmental stage. Unpublished Master's thesis, UCLA TESL Program.

Kim-Renand, Jeung Key. 1984. Personal communication, Foreign Language Department, George Mason University.

Kintch, Walter. 1977. On comprehending stories. In: Cognitive processes in comprehension. Edited by M.A. Just and P.A. Carpenter. Hillsdale, N.J.: Lawrence Erlbaum Associates.

Kintch, Walter, and J. Keenan. 1973. Reading rate and retention as a function of the number of propositions in the base structure of sentences. Cognitive Psychology 5.257-74.

Klein, W., et. al. 1979. Developmental grammars: The acquisition of German syntax by foreign workers. New York: Springer-Verlag.

Krashen, Stephen. 1978a. Is the 'natural order' an artifact of the bilingual syntax measure? Language Learning 28.175-81.

Krashen, Stephen. 1978b. The monitor model of second language acquisition. In: Second language acquisition and foreign language teaching. Edited by R. Gingras. Arlington, Va.: Center for Applied Linguistics. 1-26.

Krashen, Stephen. 1978c. Second language acquisition. In: A survey of linguistic science, 2d ed. Edited by W.O. Dingwall. Stamford, Conn.: Greylock Publishers. 317-38.

Krashen, Stephen. 1981. Second language acquisition and second language learning. Oxford: Pergamon Press.

Krashen, Stephen, F. Sterlazza, L. Feldman, and A. Fathman. 1976. Adult performance on the SLOPE test: More evidence for a natural sequence in adult second language acquisition. Language Learning 26.145-51.

Krashen, Stephen, Robin Scarcella, and Michael Long, eds. 1982. Child-adult differences in second language acquisition. Rowley, Mass.: Newbury House.

Labov, William. 1972. Sociolinguistic patterns. Philadelphia: University of Pennsylvania Press.

Labov, William. 1973. The boundaries of words and their meanings. In: New ways of analyzing variation in English. Edited by Charles-James N. Bailey and Roger W. Shuy. Washington, D.C.: Georgetown University Press. 340-73.

Labov, William. 1978. The study of nonstandard English. Urbana, Ill.: National Council of Teachers of English.

Labov, William, and Theresa Labov. 1976. Learning the syntax of questions. Paper delivered at the Conference on the Psychology of Language, Stirling, Scotland.

Lakoff, George. (forthcoming) Women, fire and other dangerous things. Chicago: University of Chicago Press.

Lakoff, George, and Mark Johnson. 1980. Metaphors we live by. Chicago: University of Chicago Press.

Larsen-Freeman, Diane. 1975. The acquisition of grammatical morphemes by adult ESL students. TESOL Quarterly 9.409-19.

Maple, R.F. 1982. Social distance and the acquisition of English as a second language: A study of Spanish-speaking adult learners. Unpublished doctoral dissertation, The University of Texas at Austin.

Maratsos, Michael. 1976. The use of definite and indefinite reference in young children. Cambridge: Cambridge University Press.

Meisel, Jurgen. 1983. Strategies of second language acquisition: More than one type of simplification. In: R. Anderson (1983:120-57).

Meisel, Jurgen, Harald Clahsen, and Manfried Pienemann. 1981. On determining developmental stages in natural second language acquisition. Studies in Second Language Acquisition 3.109-35.

Munsell, Paul, and T. Carr. 1981. Monitoring the monitor. A review of: Second language acquisition and second language learning. Language Learning 31.493-502.

Paulston, Christina, and Mary Bruder. 1976. Teaching English as a second language: Techniques and procedures. Cambridge, Mass.: Winthrop.

Pienemann, Manfred. 1984. Psycholinguistic principles of second language teaching. Unpublished MS.

Romaine, Suzanne. 1984. The language of children and adolescents. New York: Basil Blackwell.

Rosansky, Ellen. 1976. Methods and morphemes in second language acquisition. Language Learning 26.409-25.

Rosch, Eleanor. 1973. On the internal structure of perceptual and semantic categories. In: Cognitive development and the acquisition of language. Edited by T.E. Moore. New York: Academic Press. 111-44.

Rosch, Eleanor. 1975. Universals and cultural specifics in human categorization. In: Cross-cultural perspectives on learning. Edited by R. Brislin, S. Bochner, and W. Lonner. New York: Halsted Press.

Ross, John Robert. 1973. A fake NP squish. In: New ways of analyzing variation in English. Edited by Charles-James N. Bailey and Roger W. Shuy. Washington, D.C: Georgetown University Press. 96-140.

Ross, John Robert. 1974. Three batons for cognitive psychology. In: Cognitive and symbolic processes. Edited by W.B. Weimer and D. Palermo. Hillsdale, N.J.: Lawrence Erlbaum Associates. 63-124.

Ross, John Robert. 1981. Why I don't invent in Why questions, Mummy and Daddy? In: Variation omnibus. Edited by David Sankoff and Henrietta Cedergren. Carbondale, Ill.: Linguistic Research Inc. 239-48.

Sankoff, David, and William Labov. 1979. On the uses of variable rules. Language and Society 8.189-222.

Savin, H. B., and E. Perchonock. 1965. Grammatical structure and immediate recall of English sentences. Journal of Verbal Learning and Verbal Behavior 4.348-53.

Schmidt, M. 1980. Coordinate structures and language universals in interlanguage. Language Learning 30.397-416.

Schmidt, Richard. 1983. Interaction, acculturation and the acquisition of communicative competence: A case study of an adult. In: Sociolinguistics and language acquisition. Edited by N. Wolfson and E. Judd. Rowley, Mass.: Newbury House.

Schumann, John. 1978. The pidginization process. Rowley, Mass.: Newbury House.

Schumann, John. 1984. The acculturation model: The evidence. Paper presented at Symposium on Current Approaches to Second Language Acquisition, University of Wisconsin, Milwaukee, March 29-31.

Selinker, Larry. 1972. Interlanguage. International Review of Applied Linguistics 10.209-31.

Slobin, Dan. 1973. Cognitive prerequisites for the development of grammar. In: Studies of language development. Edited by Charles Ferguson and Dan Slobin. New York: Holt, Rinehart and Winston.

Smith, F. 1982. Writing and the writer. New York: Holt, Rinehart and Winston.

Stabler, E.D. 1984. Berwick and Weinberg on linguistics and computational psychology. Cognition 17.155-74.

Stampe, David. 1969. The acquisition of phonetic representation. In: Papers from the Fifth Regional Meeting of the Chicago Linguistic Society, 443-54.

Stauble, Ann Marie. 1978. The process of decreolization: A model for second language development. Language Learning 28.29-54.

Stevick, Earl. 1980. Teaching languages: A way and ways. Rowley, Mass.: Newbury House.

Tarone, Elaine. 1979. Interlanguage as chameleon. Language Learning 29.181-91.

Tarone, Elaine. 1983. On the variability of interlanguage systems. Applied Linguistics 4.142-43.

Tarone, Elaine. 1984. On the variability of interlanguage systems. In: Universals of second language acquisition. Edited by F. Eckman, L. Bell, and D. Nelson. Rowley, Mass.: Newbury House.

Tarone, Elaine. 1985. On chameleons and monitors. Paper delivered at the Second Language Research Forum, Los Angeles, February.

Traugott, Elizabeth. 1977. Natural semantax: Its role in the study of second language acquisition. In: Actes du 5eme Colloque de Linguistique Appliquee de Neuchatel. Geneva: Dooz and Universite de Neuchatel.

Valdman, Albert, ed. 1977. Pidgin and creole linguistics. Bloomington: Indiana University Press.

Wald, Benji. 1981. Limitations on the variable rule applied to bilingual phonology: The unmerging of the voiceless palatal phoneme in the English of the Mexican-Americans in the Los Angeles area. In: Variation omnibus. Edited by David Sankoff and Henrietta Cedergren. Carbondale, Ill.: Linguistic Research Inc. 215-25.

White, Lydia. 1982. Grammatical theory and language acquisition. Dordrecht: Foris Publications.

Wolfram, Walt. 1969. A sociolinguistic description of Detroit Negro speech. Washington, D.C.: Center for Applied Linguistics.

Wolfram, Walt, and Ralph Fasold. 1974. The study of social dialects in American English. Englewood Cliffs, N.J.: Prentice-Hall.